THE LIFE OF GEORGE CABOT LODGE

THE LIFE OF
GEORGE CABOT LODGE

By Henry Adams

A FACSIMILE REPRODUCTION
WITH AN INTRODUCTION BY
JOHN W. CROWLEY

SCHOLARS' FACSIMILES & REPRINTS
DELMAR, NEW YORK, 1978

SCHOLARS' FACSIMILES & REPRINTS
Series Established 1936
VOLUME 316

Published by
Scholars' Facsimiles & Reprints, Inc.
Delmar, New York 12054

First Printing 1978

New matter in this edition
©1978 John W. Crowley
All rights reserved

Printed in the United States of America

Library of Congress Cataloging in Publication Data

Adams, Henry, 1838-1918.
The life of George Cabot Lodge.

Reprint of the 1911 ed.
published by Houghton Mifflin, Boston.
1. Lodge, George Cabot, 1873-1909.
2. Poets, American—20th century—Biography.
I. Title.

PS3523.027Z6   1978   811'.4   78-16619
ISBN 0-8201-1316-6

INTRODUCTION

On August 21, 1909, George Cabot Lodge died at the age of thirty-five. Although the young poet's heart had been weakening for two years, his sudden collapse stunned his family and friends. Henry Adams had grown close to "Bay" Lodge (as friends called him), and the news plunged him into depression. "Bay was my last tie to active sympathy with men," Adams wrote to the poet's mother. "He has done enough work to place him high among the men whose names have a chance of lasting more than our day, and we can even hope that his genius may throw some rays of light on us who surround him."[1] Senator Henry Cabot Lodge believed that his son had been a great poet, and he set himself to hastening the recognition he thought Bay's poetry deserved and would eventually earn. As an immediate step, he proposed publication of the collected poems; and in the winter of 1910, when he had assembled the contents of the edition, Senator Lodge and Elizabeth Lodge, Bay's widow, asked Adams to write an official biography as part of the three-volume set.

Adams accepted the commision reluctantly. He had refused in 1905 to undertake a biography of John Hay for fear of Mrs. Hay's censorial meddling, and he expected the Lodges, despite their good intentions, to interfere. "Poor Bay's poems are to be republished in a collected form," he wrote to Elizabeth Cameron. "Bessy [Elizabeth Lodge] wants me to do a volume of Life. I assent readily, knowing that Cabot [Senator Lodge] will do it, and will not let anyone else do it, however he may try to leave it alone." Adams gathered Bay's letters and manuscripts before sailing to Paris in April, 1910. After completing half of the biography in May, he complained to

---

1. *Henry Adams and His Friends*, ed. Harold D. Cater (Boston: Houghton Mifflin, 1947), p. 662. An earlier version of this introductory essay first appeared in *New England Quarterly* 46 (June 1973).

Mrs. Cameron that he could "make nothing very good out of it."[2] Nevertheless, in October, he presented a draft to the family for approval.

As Adams had predicted, the Lodges complicated the project. Elizabeth proffered passages from Bay's love letters for use in the book but later withdrew them as too personal. Senator Lodge cavilled over genealogical details. Despite her son's pessimistic late poems, Mrs. Lodge insisted on the deletion of all "reference to failing health or discouragement" on the grounds that Bay "wanted & meant to appear at least adequate & cheerful to the world."[3] Adams, however, disavowed either suppressions or changes. "As for the MS.," he wrote Elizabeth, "it was sent to you to do what you pleased with it. That is your part of the work, with which I have nothing to do. From the moment the MS. comes into your hands, it ceases to be mine and is wholly yours."[4]

These instances of family interference illuminate such anomalies in *The Life of George Cabot Lodge* as Adams' ironic treatment of Lodge's ancestry, his handling of the Bay-Elizabeth courtship, and his dating of "The Noctambulist." Almost in parody of Biblical "begats," the first pages of *The Life* recount the family history in meticulous detail. Just as Adams' birth in the *The Education* is overshadowed by the Massachusetts statehouse, Lodge's is overshadowed by the proliferated branches of the family tree. Adams' annoyance with the Lodges' preoccupation with genealogy becomes clear later in his description of Elizabeth Lodge's background as "the usual leash of Senators, Cabinet officers, and other such ornaments, in her ancestry . . ." (p. 87). In Chapter Four, Adams asserts that Lodge's love letters "strike a note which rises high above the level of art or education"; yet he quotes only three rather insipid fragments. Several

2. *Letters of Henry Adams (1892-1918)*, ed. Worthington C. Ford (Boston: Houghton Mifflin, 1938), pp. 531, 543.

3. Letter of [Oct. 1910]. George Cabot Lodge Papers, Massachusetts Historical Society, Boston. All quotations from previously unpublished Lodge and Adams letters are by permission of the Lodge family, the Adams Papers, and the Massachusetts Historical Society.

4. Letter of Oct. 24, 1910, in the possession of Hon. Henry Cabot Lodge, Beverly, Massachusetts; hereafter, GCL Papers, Beverly.

impassioned letters had been excised at Elizabeth's request; and because he had not bothered to revise the manuscript, Adams left a residual but unintentional irony. In Chapter Eight, Adams notes that many of the poems published post-humously in Lodge's *The Soul's Inheritance* were written prior to *Herakles* (1908); but he incorrectly implies that "The Noctambulist," the pessimism of which is entirely out of key with the earlier poems, belongs to the same period. Adams feigns not to know what "change, physical or moral" (other than Lodge's grief for Trumbull Stickney) might explain the darkness of "The Noctambulist"; but he was well aware of Lodge's deteriorating health and morale after 1907, and a letter he quotes on page 201 clearly places the composition of "The Noctambulist" after *Herakles* in early 1909. In effect, to satisfy Mrs. Lodge's desire to have Lodge "appear at least adequate & cheerful to the world," Adams obfuscated the facts of Lodge's health and subordinated "The Noctambulist" to the more hopeful *Herakles*.

Adams was disturbed, however, less by the small than by the large distortions to which family pressure led, by what he perceived as the hypocrisy of the book. "Bay liked his Boston even less than I do," he reminded Elizabeth, "and we shall have trouble in trying to make this clear without using some of his own strong expressions. I foresee constant stumbling over this potato-patch; all the more because it is really the gist of the poetry. All the poems express a more or less violent reaction against Boston, and ought to be read so, if they are to be understood."[5] Of course, Henry Cabot Lodge intended the collected works and the companion biography precisely for the Boston audience Bay had rejected.

Frustrated that he could not write the iconoclastic book he and Bay would have wanted, Adams resorted to stylistic subterfuge. He would attack Boston by indirection, as he explained to Elizabeth:

> In this society made up of forms of social cowardice, we must do as Bay did,—insist on recognition,—or submit to be swamped. In this last case, we had better leave biography alone. Bay would be ashamed of us, and I should be ashamed of myself, if we deserted his standards; and the highest stan-

5. Letter of May 3, 1910. GCL Papers, Beverely.

dard he had was you.

> Yet I have so far respected the so-called American standards of taste, which are mere standards of feebleness, as to tone down the expression of my own standards to a level which seems to me flat and cold. That is not the way I should express myself if I had only myself to express. It is not the way Bay expressed himself—I can only hope that, underneath the outside form of expression, the intensity of feeling will be unconsciously there, so as to affect the average idiot without his knowing it.[6]

This letter explains the curious tone of *The Life of Lodge*, which is so ironic at times, so flat and cold, that, as Edmund Wilson observed, Adams "turns the poor young man into a shadow, and withers up his verse in a wintry pinch."[7] Adams sought to remove from the biography any trace of his friendship with and influence on Lodge. "My share in it is only to satisfy you and Bay," he wrote to Elizabeth; "and if I have allowed even a shadow of myself to come between him and his readers, I have made a mistake somewhere. I ought to be invisible; a mere mirror or . . . a slight tone of color."[8]

Adams had once warned Mrs. Lodge: "If I write it, you may be sure that it will shock you,—you know my ruthless requirement that anyone who challenges publicity, should stand up to it, and shrink from no assertion of his personality. . . ." But Adams later recognized that he had compromised his "ruthless requirement" to the "so-called American standards of taste," and he washed his hands of the book. "So Cabot came to dinner last night to talk about Bay's publication," he wrote bitterly to Mrs. Cameron; "and of course I was beautiful and approved everything, and said that I agreed with everybody, which I always do because nobody cares. Sometimes I do it once too much, as in the case of John Hay's *Letters*. Bay's will be another case of the same sort, but not so lurid. If they will only let me keep my name off it!"[9] In fact, on the pretext that "I prefer a very simple—simplest, title-page without anything that does not compel the public to think of the subject alone," Adams

6. Letter of July 29, 1910. GCL Papers, Beverly.
7. *The Shock of Recognition* (New York: Modern Library, n.d.), p. 744.
8. Letter of Oct. 25, 1911. GCL Papers, Beverly.
9. *Letters of Henry Adams*, pp. 543n., 560-61.

arranged for the publisher "to omit the author's name on the title, and rather insert it on the false title in front"[10] *The Life* was set in type in April, 1911, but delayed in publication to coincide with the October issue of *Poems and Dramas of George Cabot Lodge.* Adams disgustedly refused to think further of his involvement, as he told Mrs. Camerson: "I've made no special secret of my views about it, but I don't want myself discussed."[11]

Perhaps Adams implied in this remark an uncomfortable recognition of autobiographical elements in *The Life;* for despite Adams' efforts to make his biography "a mere mirror" of his subject, his own image is reflected as well. Increasingly, Adams had regarded Lodge as a fellow worshipper of the dynamo, as an intellectual heir capable of making the quantum leap of consciousness that would be requisite to survival in a multiverse. Adams identified himself vicariously with Lodge's youthful energy and tenacious commitment to transcending chaos in an act of mind. He surely recognized his own thoughts in this speech from Lodge's verse-drama *Herakles* (from which he quoted only the last two lines in *The Life*):

> Knowledge alone is victory! When all
> Is understood, all is subdued, received,
> Possessed and perfect. For the soul of man
> Is, in the universe of force and change,
> Of blind, immeasurable energies,
> Subtile and secret and supremely one,
> The sole self-realized power, the single strength
> Aimed and reflective and perfectible.
> Therefore alone the mind's conception turns
> Chaos to cosmos, ignorance to truth,
> Force to the freedom of articulate laws —
> Giving to phases of the senseless flux,
> One after one, the soul's identity.[12]

Adams saw in Lodge an image of himself as artist, a self capable of turning chaos to cosmos, ignorance to truth, force to the freedom of articulate laws. Thus Lodge's sudden death

10. Letter of Adams to Houghton Mifflin Company, April, 1911. Henry Cabot Lodge Papers, Massachusetts Historical Society, Boston.

11. *Letters of Henry Adams,* p. 566n.

12. *Herakles* (Boston: Houghton Mifflin, 1908), p. 269.

not only shattered Adam's future hope, but seemed to fore-
bode his own extinction as artist.

Henry James wrote to Adams shortly after Lodge's death:
"I have of him the most charming impressions & recollec-
tions. . . . I recall him as so intelligent & open & delightful—
a great and abundant social luxury."[13] Adams seized upon
this last phrase as "a portrait rather more lifelike than anything Sargent ever did. You paint even a group, for I believe
we are all now social luxuries. . . ." In 1903, Adams had described himself and James as the *type bourgeois-bostonien,*
characterized by "nervous self-consciousness[,] irritable dis-
like of America, and antipathy to Boston." Logically, the *type
bourgeois-bostonien* might become a "social luxury" to Boston; and Adams read his own fate in Lodge's. He replied
to James:

> Bay Lodge's experience last winter completed and finished
> my own. When his Herakles appeared absolutely unnoticed
> by the literary press, I regarded my thesis as demonstrated.
> Society no longer shows the intellectual life necessary to en-
> able it to react against a stimulus. My brother Brooks insists
> on the figure of paralysis. I prefer the figure of diffusion, like
> that of a river falling into an ocean. Either way, it drowned
> Bay, and has left me still floating, with vast curiosity to see
> what vaster absence of curiosity can bring about in my Sar-
> gasso sea.[14]

Adams feared that the ocean which had drowned Lodge cir-
cumscribed his Sargasso Sea, and the writing of *The Life*
became self-portraiture in the guise of biography. Rather
than erasing himself from the book, as he had told Elizabeth
Lodge, he obliquely cast himself as its protagonist.

The similarities of style, structure, and tone of *The Life of
Lodge* to *The Education of Henry Adams* are too numerous
to be coincidental. As Ernest Samuels has remarked, "In the
letters that Adams selected Lodge seems at times almost a
mirror image of his biographer." George Hochfield has ar-
gued further that *The Life* "can be read as a supplemen-
tal autobiography or retrospect of his own life through the

13. Letter of Aug. 31, 1909. Henry Adams Papers, Massachusetts Historical Society, Boston; see *Letters of Henry Adams,* p. 522n.

14. *Letters of Henry Adams,* pp. 522, 414.

medium of someone else's."[15] Unable to portray Lodge as he was, Adams transformed him into a *persona* of the *type bourgeois-bostonien* and depersonalized Lodge's life into a metaphor of his own artistic defeat. The life of the poet became a vehicle for Adams' real theme, anticipated in his letter to James: the impossibility of the artist's survival either inside or outside Boston culture.

In the context of Adams' late essays—*The Rule of Phase Applied to History* and *A Letter to American Teachers of History*—*The Life of Lodge* may be read as evidence of social entropy. The opening chapter depicts a Boston in which cultural energy has dissipated, perhaps in accordance with the Second Law of Thermodynamics: "A poet, born in Boston, in 1873, saw about him a society which commonly bred refined tastes, and often did refined work, but seldom betrayed strong emotions. The excitements of war had long passed; its ideals were forgotten, and no other great ideal had followed. The twenty-five years between 1873 and 1898 —years of astonishing scientific and mechanical activity— were marked by a steady decline of literary and artistic intensity, and especially of the feeling for poetry . . ." (p. 6). The last generation of famous New England writers was dead or dying; and young Lodge cultivated his talent in an atmosphere devoid of the "the classic and promiscuous turmoil of the forum, the theatre, or the bath, which trained the Greeks and the Romans, or the narrower contact of the church and the coffee-house, which bred the polished standards of Dryden and Racine." Adams assumes ironically that Lodge's poetic aptitude must have been congenital because Boston's was not a culture that "could have inspired a taste for poetry." In fact, for the Bostonian, "poetry was a suppressed instinct" that naturally took form as a "reaction against society" (pp. 7-9).

The famous contrast in *The Education* between cold, urban, hostile Boston and warm, pastoral, liberating Quincy is echoed in *The Life* in terms of Lodge's winters in Boston and summers at Nahant, where Lodge learned to feel "the sea as

15. Samuels, *Henry Adams: The Major Phase* (Cambridge: Harvard University Press, 1964), p. 503; Hochfield, *Henry Adams: An Introduction and Interpretation* (New York: Barnes & Noble, 1962), p. 141.

an echo or double of himself." According to Adams, Lodge's
nature "was itself as elementary and simple as the salt
water"; his mind "was never complex, and the complexities
merely gathered on it, as something outside, like the sea-
weeds gathering and swaying about the rocks" (pp. 11-12).
Comparing Lodge to a "Norse faun," Adams contends that
because Lodge was incapable of "finding nature perverse
and unintelligible," he necessarily concluded that "immo-
rality and futility must be in the mind": "Man became an
outrage, — society an artificial device for the distortion of
truth, — civilization a wrong" (p. 12).

Adams rejects Lodge's conclusions as simplistic and ultimately suicidal: "Many millions of simple natures have
thought, and still think, the same thing, and the more complex have never quite made up their minds whether to agree
with them or not; but the thought that was simple and
sufficient for the Norseman exploring the tropics, or for an
exuberant young savage sailing his boat off the rude shores
of Gloucester and Cape Ann, could not long survive in the
atmosphere of State Sreet. Commonly the poet dies young"
(pp. 12-13). As I have shown elsewhere,[16] Adams' characteri-
zation of Lodge is reductive; but it suits Adams' purpose in
The Life. By casting Lodge as naive, Adams purges his own
sympathy for blaming society's ills on civilization and then
withdrawing in self-righteous rebellion. Because Adams as
scientific-historian was resigned to the hegemony of cosmic
forces, and Adams as citizen was determined to survive in
the atmosphere of State Street, he could not endorse Lodge's
"savage" ideas; but he continued to envy Lodge's solution
of withdrawal.

The theme of tension between immersion in the life of
State Street and withdrawal from it was adumbrated in
Adams' poem, "Buddha and Brahma," written in 1891 under
the influence of his travels to the Orient.[17] "Buddha and
Brahma" concerns a youth torn between the examples of his
father, the Rajah, and his teacher, Buddha. At the beginning
of the poem, the youth Malunka asks his master Buddha if

16. George Cabot Lodge (Boston: Twayne, 1976).

17. Quotations are taken from A Henry Adams Reader, ed. Elizabeth
Stevenson (Garden City, N.Y.: Anchor, 1959), pp. 332-38.

the world exists eternally. Buddha ignores the question until Malunka asks it a third time. Finally, in response, Buddha raises silently the lotus he holds in his hand. Mystified by this sign, the boy looks to his father for interpretation. The Rajah, a Brahmin rather than a follower of Buddha, is "Famous for human wisdom, subtle counsel,/ Boldness in action, recklessness in war." He insists that because his life of action is contrary to Buddha's contemplative way, he cannot explain the sign; and he defines the differences between his life of immersion and Buddha's life of withdrawal. He recalls that in youth both he and Buddha rebelled in contrary ways against the priesthood and the rules of caste:

> We sought new paths, desperate to find escape
> Out of the jungle that the priests had made.
> Gautama [Buddha] found a path. You follow it.
> I found none, and I stay here, in the jungle,
> Content to tolerate what I cannot mend.

From the Rajah's point of view, Buddha escaped the jungle only by flight from life's cares:

> He failed to cope with life; renounced its cares;
> Fled to the forest, and attained the End,
> Reaching the End by sacrificing life.

Burdened with administering his realm and defending his people, the Rajah could not evade so easily the responsibilities of life. He feels, nevertheless, that Buddha's way is best if escape is possible;

> But we, who cannot fly the world, must seek
> To live two separate lives; one, in the world
> Which we must ever seem to treat as real;
> The other in ourselves, behind a veil
> Not to be raised without disturbing both.

For the Rajah, who seems to speak for Adams in the poem, the life of immersion and the life of withdrawal are polarities that the wise man can try to resolve only by living a double life: as Brahmin in society, as Buddhist in private. But the wise man must recognize that the two modes are irreconcilable; within the jungle of society, the Rajah must covet the Perfect Life in silence:

> Thus in the life of Ruler, Warrior, Master,
> The wise man knows his wisdom has no place,
> And when most wise, we act by rule and law,

> Talk to conceal our thought, and think
> Only within the range of daily need,
> Ruling our subjects while ourselves rebel,
> Death always on our lips and in our act.

Like the Rajah, Adams is unable to follow the path of contemplative withdrawal but equally unable to forget its attractions.

In *The Life of Lodge,* this tension between immersion and withdrawal recurs in Adams' analysis of Lodge's Creon and Herakles. Creon, according to Adams, is "the man-of-the-world, the administrator, the humorist and sage, who has accepted all the phases of life, and has reached the end, which he also accepts . . ." (pp. 166-67). Creon bequeaths his crown to Herakles, who rebukes him for his worldliness and renounces the throne to fulfill his other-worldly mission. Herakles represents for Lodge the heroic poet-prophet, who embraces the divine paradox of forsaking human society in order to save humankind. Adams appears sympathetic to what he calls the "superhuman solution" of Herakles; but he sees as much of himself in worldly Creon who, like the Rajah, cannot escape social responsibilities. In fact, on the choice between Creon and Herakles, Adams is mordantly equivocal:

> Not only philosophers, but also, and particularly, society it-self, for many thousands of years, have waged bloody wars over these two solutions of the problem . . . But while neither solution has ever been universally accepted as convincing, that of Herakles has at least the advantage of being as old as the oldest, and as new as the newest philosophy . . . Paradox for paradox, the only alternative—Creon's human solution—is on the whole rather more paradoxical, and certainly less logical, than the superhuman solution of Herakles. (pp. 181-82)

In *The Life,* Adams recapitulates the theme of "Buddha and Brahma": the antinomy of immersion in multiplicity (Rajah, Creon, Adams as narrator of *The Life*) and withdrawal from it (Buddha, Herakles, Lodge as *persona* in *The Life*). But if the tone of "Buddha and Brahma" is stoical, the tone of *The Life* is nihilistic. The darkening of Adams' vision results from his identification of the life of withdrawal with the suicidal life of the artist in revolt.

Adams notes in *The Life* that the instinct to rebel against society became commonplace among nineteenth-century Ro-

mantic poets; and he places Lodge in a tradition of dissent
which included Byron, Shelley, Swinburne, Verlaine, and
Whitman. But, Adams remarks, to the average Bostonian
"absorbed in the extremely practical problem of effecting
some sort of working arrangement between Beacon Street
and the universe, the attitude of revolt seemed unnatural
and artificial" (pp. 15-16). Lodge's education is shown to
have been as antiquated as the eighteenth-century education of Henry Adams; Lodge failed to recognize the obsoles-
cence of rebellion:

> The gap between the poet and the citizen was so wide as to
> be impassable in Boston, but it was not a division of society
> into hostile camps, as it had been in England with Shelley and
> Keats, or in Boston itself, half a century before, with the anti-
> slavery outbursts of Emerson and Whittier, Longfellow and
> Lowell, which shook the foundations of the State. The Bos-
> tonian of 1900 differed from his parents and grandparents of
> 1850, in owning nothing the value of which, in the market,
> could be affected by the poet. Indeed, to him, the poet's pose
> of hostility to actual conditions of society was itself mercan-
> tile, — a form of drama, — a thing to sell, rather than a serious
> revolt. Society could safely adopt it as a form of industry, as
> it adopted other forms of book-making. (pp. 16-17)

Boston culture, too effete even to recoil under the poet's
attack, co-opts him by turning his art into merchandise, and
ultimately leaves him without an audience: "Society was not
disposed to defend itself from criticism or attack. Indeed, the
most fatal part of the situation for the poet in revolt, the
paralyzing drug that made him helpless, was that society no
longer seemed sincerely to believe in itself or anything else;
it resented nothing, not even praise. The young poet grew up
without being able to find an enemy" (p. 17).

The Education of Henry Adams may be interpreted as a
triumph of form; unity is forged from multiplicity in Adams'
creation of his "Supreme Fiction," the Dynamic Theory of
History. David L. Minter, for example, argues that this imaginative construct "may 'justly' be called 'a work of art'; for,
as an effort at supreme order and as a labor of inclusive
affirmation, it constitutes its maker's ultimate act of life, his
final adherence to 'the principle of resistance.' "[18] In this

18. *The Interpreted Design as a Structural Principle in American Prose*

view, Adams' failures as historian (his *persona* in *The Education*) are redeemed by his victory as artist. As artist, Adams
manages to reconcile his vision of chaos with his psychic
need for unity: "The secret of education still hid itself somewhere behind ignorance, and one fumbled over it as feebly
as ever. In such labyrinths, the staff is a force almost more
necessary than the legs; the pen becomes a sort of blind-
man's dog, to keep him from falling into the gutters. The pen
works for itself, and acts like a hand, modelling the plastic
material over and over again to the form that suits it best.
The form is never arbitrary, but is a sort of growth like
crystallization, as any artist knows too well. . . ."[19]

Read as a coda to *The Education, The Life of Lodge* denies
the shaping power of imagination that Adams affirms in *The
Education. The Life* demonstrates that, despite its attractions, the life of the artist, especially of the *type bourgeois-
bostonien,* leads to suffocation in the modern wasteland:

> However much he [Lodge] tried, and the more he tried, to
> lessen the gap between himself—his group of personal friends
> —and the public, the gap grew steadily wider; the circle of
> sympathies enlarged itself not at all, or with desperate slow-
> ness; and this consciousness of losing ground,—of failure to
> find a larger horizon of friendship beyond his intimacy;—the
> growing fear that, beyond this narrow range, no friends ex-
> isted in the immense void of society—or could exist, in the
> form of society which he lived in,—the suffocating sense of
> talking and singing in a vacuum that allowed no echo to re-
> turn, grew more and more oppressive with each effort to over-
> come it. (p. 145)

Adams might have been speaking for himself here; and, so
far as Adams identified himself with Lodge as an artist of
the *type bourgeois-bostonien, The Life* was an act of self-
annihilation.

The depth of Adams' pessimism about the future of the
artist in America is suggested by a letter he wrote to Elizabeth Cameron after Lodge's death: "Edith Wharton's notice
[on Lodge, published in *Scribner's Magazine,* February,1910]
is very nicely done . . . but all the notices from today to

(New Haven: Yale University Press, 1969), p. 133.

19. *The Education of Henry Adams,* ed. Ernest Samuels (Boston: Houghton Mifflin, 1973), p. 389.

doomsday will never make an American public care for poetry,—or anything else unless perhaps chewing-gum."[20] The alternative to "singing in a vacuum" seemed to be living in an entropic culture. Damned either way, Adams despaired of any "larger synthesis" except one in which all contradictions would be resolved only in a larger contradiction.

JOHN W. CROWLEY

Syracuse University

20. *Letters of Henry Adams*, p. 531.

THE LIFE OF

GEORGE CABOT LODGE

BY HENRY ADAMS

THE LIFE

OF

GEORGE CABOT LODGE

BOSTON AND NEW YORK
HOUGHTON MIFFLIN COMPANY
1911

CONTENTS

THE LIFE OF
GEORGE CABOT LODGE

CHAPTER I

CHILDHOOD

POETS are proverbially born, not made; and, because they have been born rarely, the conditions of their birth are singularly interesting. One imagines that the conditions surrounding the birth of New England poets can have varied little, yet, in shades, these conditions differ deeply enough to perplex an artist who does not know where to look for them. Especially the society of Boston has always believed itself to have had, from the start, a certain complexity, — certain rather refined *nuances*, — which gave it an avowed right to stand apart; a right which its members never hesitated to assert, if it pleased them to do so, and which no one thought of questioning. One of the best-known and most strongly marked of these numerous families, was — and still is — that of the Cabots, whose early story has been told by Henry Cabot Lodge in his life of the best-known member of the family, his great-grandfather, George Cabot, Senator of the United States.

George Cabot's son Henry married Anna Blake, and had a daughter, Anna Sophia Cabot, who married John Ellerton Lodge. The Lodges were new arrivals in Boston. Giles Lodge, the grandfather, having narrowly escaped with his life from the San Domingo massacre, arrived, a young Englishman and a stranger, in Boston in 1791. There he established himself in business and married Mary Langdon, daughter of John Langdon, an officer of the Continental Army and cousin of President Langdon of Harvard College, who prayed for the troops on the eve of Bunker Hill. Through his mother John Lodge was descended from the Walleys and Brattles and other Puritan families of Boston, now for the most part extinct and forgotten. But despite the paternal grandmother, Henry Cabot Lodge, the only son of John

Ellerton Lodge and Anna Cabot, felt himself Bostonian chiefly on the mother's side, as an off-shoot of the prolific stock of the Cabots, who were really all of Essex County origin. He marked the point by making for himself a world-wide reputation under the double name of Cabot Lodge. Of him the public needs no biography, since he became a familiar figure to millions of his fellow-citizens from somewhat early youth to a fairly advanced age; and, from the conspicuous stage of the United States Senate, offered a far more conspicuous presence than his great-grandfather, George Cabot, had ever done.

To Bostonians, in general, the Cabots altogether are a stock too strong, too rich, too varied in their family characteristics, to need explanation. Volumes might be written on them, without exhausting the varieties of the strain.

That such a family should produce a poet was not matter for surprise; but as though to make such a product quite natural and normal, Henry Cabot Lodge, who was born May 12, 1850, married, on June 29, 1871, into another Massachusetts family

with history and characteristics as marked as those
of the Cabots themselves.

The Plymouth Colony produced Davises as
freely as the north shore produced Cabots. Daniel
Davis, of the Barnstaple stock, was Solicitor-General
of Massachusetts in the days, about 1800,
when the Reverend James Freeman was the Unitarian
minister of King's Chapel; and Daniel Davis
married Lois Freeman, who bore him thirteen children.
The oldest, Louisa, married William Minot,
of a family more thoroughly Bostonian, if possible,
than all the rest. The youngest, Charles Henry
Davis, born January 16, 1807, in Somerset Street,
Boston, and, in due course, sent to Harvard College,
left the College, in 1823, to enter the navy as
midshipman, in order to cruise in the old frigate,
the United States, in the Pacific, under the command
of his friend and patron, Commodore Isaac
Hull.

The life of Admiral Davis has been admirably
told elsewhere, and his victories at Hilton Head,
in November, 1861, at Fort Pillow, in May, 1862,
at Memphis and Vicksburg, afterwards, rank

among the most decisive of the Civil War, as they
rank also among the earliest to give some share of
hope or confidence to the national government and
to the loyal voters; but his brilliant career in the
navy concerns his grandson-poet less than the domestic event of his marriage, in 1842, to Harriette
Blake Mills, daughter of still another United
States Senator, Elijah Hunt Mills, of Northamp-
ton, Massachusetts, who was also a conspicuous
figure in his day.

The complications of this alliance were curious,
and among them was the chance that another
daughter of Senator Mills married Benjamin
Peirce, the famous Professor of Mathematics at
Harvard College, so that the children of Admiral
Davis became first cousins of the great mathema-
tician Charles Peirce and his brothers. Among
these children of Admiral Davis was a daughter,
Anna Cabot Mills Davis, who grew up to girlhood
in Cambridge, under the shadow of Harvard College, where her father, the Admiral, lived while not
in active service; and when, after his appointment
to the Naval Observatory, he transferred his resi-

dence to Washington, she made her home there until her marriage, in June, 1871, to Henry Cabot Lodge.

Her second child, George Cabot Lodge, the subject of this story, was born in Boston, October 10, 1873.

A poet, born in Boston, in 1873, saw about him a society which commonly bred refined tastes, and often did refined work, but seldom betrayed strong emotions. The excitements of war had long passed; its ideals were forgotten, and no other great ideal had followed. The twenty-five years between 1873 and 1898 — years of astonishing scientific and mechanical activity — were marked by a steady decline of literary and artistic intensity, and especially of the feeling for poetry, which, at best, had never been the favorite form of Boston expression. The only poet who could be called strictly Bostonian by birth, — Ralph Waldo Emerson, — died in the year 1882, before young Lodge was ten years old. Longfellow, who always belonged to Cambridge rather than to Boston, died in the same year. James Russell

Lowell survived till 1891, but was also in no strict social sense a Bostonian. Young men growing up on Beacon Hill or the Back Bay never met such characters unless by a rare chance; and as the city became busier and more crowded, the chances became rarer still.

Not the society, therefore, could have inspired a taste for poetry. Such an instinct must have been innate, like his cousin's mathematics. Society could strike him only as the absence of all that he might have supposed it to be, as he read of it in the history and poetry of the past. Even since the youth of R. W. Emerson, the sense of poetry had weakened like the sense of religion. Boston differed little from other American towns with less reputation for intellect, where, as a rule, not many persons entered their neighbors' houses, and these were members of the family. A stranger was unknown.

The classic and promiscuous turmoil of the forum, the theatre, or the bath, which trained the Greeks and the Romans, or the narrower contact of the church and the coffee-house, which bred the polished standards of Dryden and Racine, were unknown in America, and nearly extinct in Paris and London. An American boy scarcely conceived of getting social education from contact with his elders. In previous generations he had been taught to get it from books, but the young American of this period was neither a bookish nor a social animal. Climate and custom combined to narrow his horizon.

Commonly the boy was well pleased to have it so; he asked only to play with his fellows, and to escape contact with the world; but the Boston child of the Cabot type was apt to feel himself alone even as a child. Unless singularly fortunate in finding and retaining sympathetic companions, his strong individuality rebelled against its surroundings. Boys are naturally sensitive and shy. Even as men, a certain proportion of society showed, from the time of the Puritans, a marked reserve, so that one could never be quite sure in State Street, more than in Concord, that the lawyer or banker whom one consulted about drawing a deed or negotiating a loan, might not be uncon-

sciously immersed in introspection, as his ances-
tors, two centuries before, had been absorbed in
their chances of salvation. The latent contrasts of
character were full of interest, and so well understood that any old Bostonian, familiar with family
histories, could recall by scores the comedies and
tragedies which had been due to a conscious or
unconscious revolt against the suppression of instinct and imagination.

Poetry was a suppressed instinct: and except
where, as in Longfellow, it kept the old character
of ornament, it became a reaction against society,
as in Emerson·and the Concord school, or, further
away and more roughly, in Walt Whitman. Less
and less it appeared, as in earlier ages, the natural, favorite expression of society itself. In the
last half of the nineteenth century, the poet became everywhere a rebel against his surroundings.
What had been begun by Wordsworth, Byron, and
Shelley, was carried on by Algernon Swinburne
in London or Paul Verlaine in Paris or Walt
Whitman in Washington, by a common instinct
of revolt. Even the atmosphere of Beacon

Street was at times faintly redolent of Schopenhauer.

The tendency of Bostonians to break away from
conventional society was fostered by the harshness
of the climate, but was vastly helped by the neigh-
borhood of the ocean. Snow and ice and fierce
northwest gales shut up society within doors during three months of winter; while equally fierce
heat drove society to camp within tide-water, during three months of summer. There the ocean was
the closest of friends. Every one knows the little
finger of granite that points oceanward, some ten
miles north of Boston, as though directing the
Bostonian homeward. The spot is almost an
island, connected with Lynn by a long, narrow
strip of sand-beach; but on the island a small
township called Nahant has long existed, and the
end of this point of Nahant was bought by the
grandfather, John Ellerton Lodge, as a country-
place for summer residence.

The whole coast, for five hundred miles in either
direction, has since been seized for summer residence, but Nahant alone seems to be actually the

ocean itself, as though it were a ship quitting
port, or, better, just stranded on the rocky coast of
Cape Ann. There the winds and waves are alone
really at home, and man can never by day or night
escape their company. At the best of times, and
in their most seductive temper, their restlessness
carries a suggestion of change, — a warning of
latent passion, — a threat of storm. One looks out
forever to an infinite horizon of shoreless and
shifting ocean.

The sea is apt to revive some primitive instinct
in boys, as though in a far-off past they had been
fishes, and had never quite forgotten their home.
The least robust can feel the repulsion, even when
they cannot feel the physical attraction, of the
waves playing with the rocks like children never
quite sure of their temper; but the Lodge boy, like
most other boys of his class and breed, felt the sea
as an echo or double of himself. Commonly this
instinct of unity with nature dies early in American life; but young Lodge's nature was itself as elementary and simple as the salt water. Throughout
life, the more widely his character spread in cir-

cumference, the more simply he thought, and even
when trying to grow complex, — as was inevitable
since it was to grow in Boston, — the mind itself
was never complex, and the complexities merely
gathered on it, as something outside, like the sea-
weeds gathering and swaying about the rocks.
Robust in figure, healthy in appetite, careless of
consequences, he could feel complex and intro-
spective only as his ideal, the Norse faun, might
feel astonished and angry at finding nature perverse and unintelligible in a tropical jungle. Since
nature could not be immoral or futile, the immor-
ality and futility must be in the mind that conceived it. Man became an outrage, — society an
artificial device for the distortion of truth, — civilization a wrong. Many millions of simple natures
have thought, and still think, the same thing, and
the more complex have never quite made up their
minds whether to agree with them or not; but the
thought that was simple and sufficient for the
Norseman exploring the tropics, or for an exuberant young savage sailing his boat off the rude
shores of Gloucester and Cape Ann, could not long

survive in the atmosphere of State Street. Commonly the poet dies young.

The Nahant life was intensely home, with only a father and mother for companions, an elder sister, a younger brother, cousins or boy friends at hazard, and boundless sea and sky. As the boy passed his tenth year, his father — possibly inspired by the same spirit of restlessness — turned much of his time and attention to politics, and the mother became all the more the companion and resource of the children. From the earliest forms of mammal life, the mothers of fauns have been more in love with their offspring than with all else in existence; and when the mother has had the genius of love and sympathy, the passion of altruism, the instinct of taste and high-breeding, besides the commoner resources of intelligence and education, the faun returns the love, and is moulded by it into shape.

These were the elements of his youth, and the same elements will be found recurring in all that he thought and said during his thirty-six years of life. He was himself, both in fact and in imagination, "The Wave," whose song he began his literary career by composing: —

This is the song of the wave, that died in the fulness of life.
The prodigal this, that lavished its largess of strength
In the lust of achievement.
Aiming at things for Heaven too high,
Sure in the pride of life, in the richness of strength.
So tried it the impossible height, till the end was found,
Where ends the soul that yearns for the fillet of morning stars,
The soul in the toils of the journeying worlds,
Whose eye is filled with the image of God,
    And the end is Death.

Had the "Song of the Wave" been written after death instead of before the beginning of life, the figure could not have been more exact. The young man felt the image as he felt the act; his thought offered itself to him as a wave. From first to last he identified himself with the energies of nature, as the story will show; he did not invent images for amusement, but described himself in describing the energy. Even the figure of the Norse faun was his own figure, and like the Wave, with which it belongs, was an effort at the first avowal of him-

self to himself; for these things were of his youth,
felt and not feigned: —

> These are the men!
> The North has given them name,
> The children of God who dare. . . .
> These are the men!
> In their youth without memory
> They were glad, for they might not see
> The lies that the world has wrought
> On the parchment of God. The tree
> Yielded them ships, and the sky
> 'Flamed as the waters fought;
> But they knew that death was a lie,
> That the life of man was as nought,
> And they dwelt in the truth of the sea.
> These are the men.

In conditions of life less intimate than those of
Boston, such a way of conceiving one's own existence seems natural; indeed almost normal for
Wordsworths and Byrons, Victor Hugos and Wal-
ter Savage Landors, Algernon Swinburnes and
Robert Louis Stevensons; — but to the Bostonian
absorbed in the extremely practical problem of
effecting some sort of working arrangement be-

tween Beacon Street and the universe, the attitude
of revolt seemed unnatural and artificial. He could
not even understand it. For centuries the Bostonian had done little but wrestle with nature for
a bare existence, and his foothold was not so secure,
nor had it been so easily acquired, nor was it so
victoriously sufficient for his wants, as to make
him care to invite the ice or the ocean once more to
cover it or himself; while, even more keenly than
the Scotchman or Norseman, he felt that he ought
not to be reproached for the lies that the world,
including himself, had wrought, under compulsion,
on the e. .eedingly rough and scanty parchment of
God.

The efore the gap between the poet and the citizen was so wide as to be impassable in Boston, but
it was not a division of society into hostile camps,
as it had been in England with Shelley and Keats,
or in Boston itself, half a century before, with the
anti-slavery outbursts of Emerson and Whittier,
Longfellow and Lowell, which shook the founda-
tions of the State. The Bostonian of 1900 differed
from his parents and grandparents of 1850, in own-

ing nothing the value of which, in the market, could be affected by the poet. Indeed, to him, the poet's pose of hostility to actual conditions of society was itself mercantile, — a form of drama, — a thing to sell, rather than a serious revolt. Society could safely adopt it as a form of industry, as it adopted other forms of book-making.

Therefore, while, for young Lodge and other protestants of his age and type, the contrast between Nahant and Beacon Street was a real one, — even a vital one, — life in both places was normal, healthy, and quite free from bitterness or social strain. Society was not disposed to defend itself from criticism or attack. Indeed, the most fatal part of the situation for the poet in revolt, the paralyzing drug that made him helpless, was that society no longer seemed sincerely to believe in itself or anything else; it resented nothing, not even praise. The young poet grew up without being able to find an enemy. With a splendid physique, a warmly affectionate nature, a simple but magnificent appetite for all that life could give, a robust indifference or defiance of consequences, a social position unconscious of dispute or doubt, and a large, insatiable ambition to achieve ideals, — with these ample endowments and energies, in full consciousness of what he was about to attempt, the young man entered deliberately upon what he was to call his Great Adventure.

CHAPTER II

CAMBRIDGE AND PARIS

To all young Bostonians of a certain age and social position, Harvard College opens its doors so genially as to impose itself almost as a necessary path into the simple problems of Boston life; and it has the rather unusual additional merit of offering as much help as the student is willing to accept towards dealing with the more complex problems of life in a wider sense. Like most of his friends and family, young Lodge, at eighteen years old, went to the University, and profited by it in his own way, which was rarely, with Bostonians of his type, precisely the way which the actual standards of American life required or much approved. The first two years seldom profit young men of this class at all, but with the third year, their tastes, if they have any, begin to show themselves, and their minds grope for objects that offer them attraction, or for supports that the young tendrils can grasp. Every instructor has seen this rather blind process going on in generation after generation of students, and is seldom able to lend much help to it; but if he is so fortunate as to teach some subject that attracts the student's fancy, he can have influence. Owing to some innate sympathies, which were apparently not due to inheritance or conditions, Lodge seemed to care less for English than for French or Italian or classic standards; and it happened that the French department was then directed by Professor Bôcher, who took a fancy to the young man, and not only helped him to an acquaintance with the language, but still more with the literature and the thought of France, a subject in which Professor Bôcher was an admirable judge and critic.

At first, the student made the usual conscientious effort to do what did not amuse him. "I am going to acquire the faculty of not minding applying myself to uninteresting subjects, if I can, and I am sure that it is possible," he wrote to his mother, March 21, 1893; and then, pursuing the usual course which started most Harvard students on literary careers, he fell at once into the arms of Thomas Carlyle. "I am making a study of the religious and philosophical side of Carlyle, with a view to writing a book on the same; and it is a most absorbing subject," he wrote on May 6, 1893. "My head is full of ideas which I want to let out in that book. I propose to devote my summer to it. Even if it is n't a success, it is better than doing nothing, and it is profoundly interesting. I have read attentively almost everything he ever wrote except 'Cromwell,' and I am taking notes on all the more philosophical ones, like 'Sartor Resartus'; and I am also reading and studying conjointly the French philosophers, Descartes, Malebranche and Spinoza, and the German Schopenhauer and Fichte, and also Plato, so that I shall get an idea of his relations to the celebrated philosophies. I am going to read Froude's life of him." The door by which a student enters the vast field of philosophy matters little, for, whatever it is, the student cannot stay long in it; but for one of such wide views, Carlyle could serve a very short time as the central interest.

"To-day Bourget came out here to a lecture in French 7 by Sumichrast, and Sumichrast got him to talk, which he did most charmingly. I have been taking a course of Bourget, among other things, 'Mensonges'; and I feel as if I had been living in the mire. Never have I read books whose atmosphere was so unhealthy and fetid." This was written to his mother, December 12, 1893, when he was barely twenty years old, and marks the steady tide of French influence that was carrying him on to its usual stage of restlessness and depression. On February 28, 1894, he wrote again, announcing that he had fairly reached the moral chaos which belonged to his temperament and years: "I am in very good health and very bad spirits, and I am feeling pretty cynical. It is a constant struggle for me to prevent myself from becoming cynical, and when I feel blue and depressed, the dykes break and it all comes to the surface. I suppose I have seen more of the evil and mean side of men and things than most men of my age, which accounts for my having naturally a pessimistic turn. Really, though, I hate cynicism; — it is a compilation of cheap aphorisms that any fool can learn to repeat; — and yet the world does seem a bad place."

A common place rather than a bad place was the next natural and cheap aphorism which every imaginative young man could look with confidence to reach, but the process of reaching it varies greatly with the temperament of the men. In Lodge it soon took the form of philosophic depression accompanied by intense ambition. The combination, at the age of twenty, is familiar in Europeans, but not so common among Americans, who are apt to feel, or to show, diffidence in their own powers. Lodge's letters will reveal himself fully on that side, but what they show still better is the immense appetite of the young man for his intellectual food, once he had found the food he liked.

"Since I got back [to Cambridge]," he wrote to his mother on March 14, 1894, "I have been reading an immense quantity from variegated authors, Balzac especially; also Flaubert, Alfred de Vigny, Leconte de Lisle, and Musset, Hugo, Renan (whom I am going to write a long French theme about), Schopenhauer, and then the Upanishads, etc. Next time French literature is discussed, ask them what living poet equals Sully Prudhomme." He was already in a region where Boston society — or indeed, any other society except perhaps that of Paris — would have been puzzled to answer his questions; but the sense of reaching new regions excited him. "I am beginning to get beautifully into harness now," he wrote on November 16, 1894, "and find that, outside my College work, I can read from one hundred and fifty to two hundred pages a day. . . . If I were living in Gobi or Sahara, with the British Museum next door and the Louvre round the corner, I think I could do almost anything. When I work I have to fill myself full of my subject, and then write everything down without referring to any books. If I am interrupted in the agonies of composition, it takes me some time to get into the vein." The passion for reading passed naturally into the passion for writing, and every new volume read reflected itself in a volume to be written. The last term of college began and ended in this frame of mind. He wrote on January 17, 1895: "I have a scheme of writing essays on Schopenhauer, Swift, Molière, Poe, Leconte de Lisle, Carlyle, Alfred de Vigny, Balzac, Thackeray (perhaps) and any others I may think of, and entitling the collection 'Studies in Pessimism,' or some such title, and treat them all, of course, from that point of view. I could write them all except Swift and Thackeray and Balzac with very little preparation; and even with those three I should not need much. I wish you would ask papa what he thinks of my idea. Last night Max Scull and I took Brun (the French teacher) to dinner and the theatre afterwards. He was quite entertaining, and I improved my French considerably, as we spoke nothing else. I told him I was going to France next summer, and he told me to write to him and 'qu' il me montrerait Paris à fond.' I have been working on my wretched story, and have gone over it about 8 times. It now seems to me to be quite valueless. Also I have burst into song several times — rather lamely, I fear."

Then began, still in college, the invariable,

never-ending effort of the artist to master his art,
— to attain the sureness of hand and the quality
of expression which should be himself. Lodge
plunged into the difficulties with the same appetite which he felt for the facilities of expression,
and felt at once where his personal difficulties
were likely to be greatest, in his own exuberance.
"I find I cannot polish my verses to any great extent," he continued on March 20, 1895; "I write
when I feel in the mood, and then they are done —
badly or well, as the case may be. If badly, they
must either be all written over, or else burnt, and a
new one written, generally the most appropriate
fate for most of them. However, I am indeed very
glad that you and papa think I am improving,
however slightly. I enclose three efforts in a more
lyrical strain. I find it rather a relief to be less
trammeled, and unfettered to so concrete and absolute a form as the Petrarchan sonnet, — which
is the only kind I write now. I have been looking
over the few sonnets Shelley wrote. He had no
form at all in them. He seems to have built them
up with no preconceived idea of form whatever.

Take 'Ozymandias' for instance, which I admire intensely, and one finds no structure at all. Yet of course we know that the whole, as read, is superb. I wonder if most people notice the form of a sonnet. I know I did n't, before I began to scribble myself. Still, I do think, other things being equal, that the Petrarchan form adds a dignity and beauty to a sonnet which no other form possesses. The contour is much more harmonious and symmetrical."

Thus the young man had plunged headlong into the higher problems of literary art, before he was fairly acquainted with the commoner standards. Whether he ever framed to himself a reason for pursuing one form rather than another, might be a curious question. Why should not Shakespeare and the Elizabethans have appealed to him first? Was it because the Petrarchan form was more perfect, or because it was less English? Whatever the answer to this question may be, the fact is that, throughout life, he turned away from the English models, and seemed often indifferent to their existence. The trait was not wholly peculiar to him, for even in England itself the later Victorian poets, with Algernon Swinburne at their head, showed a marked disposition to break rather abruptly with the early Victorian poets, and to wander away after classical or mediæval standards; but their example was hardly the influence that affected Lodge. With him, the English tradition possibly represented a restraint,—a convention,—a chain that needed to be broken, — that jarred on his intense ambition.

"Oh, I am devoured by ambition," he wrote in the last days of his college life, to his mother: "I do so want to do something that will last,—some man's work in the world, — that I am constantly depressed by an awful dread that perhaps I shan't be able to. I am never satisfied with what I do, — never contented with my expression of what I wish to express, and yet I hope and sometimes feel that it is possible I may do something permanent in value. I have got at last a scheme for the future which I think it probable you will like, and papa also; but I shall be better able to tell you when I see you. I have read nothing lately outside my work except the 'Theologia Germanica' which Mrs. Wintie [Chanler] sent me, and which has many beautiful things in it. I have written even less,—just a few scraps of verse (one of which, a sonnet, is coming out in the next 'Monthly' by the way), and that article on Shakespeare which went to papa. I am anxious to know what he thinks of it."

With this, the college life closed, having given, liberally and sympathetically, all it could give, leaving its graduates free, and fairly fitted, to turn where they chose for their further food; which meant, for young Lodge, as his letters have told, the immediate turning to Paris. The choice showed the definite determination of his thought. England, Germany, Italy, did not, at that stage, offer the kind of education he wanted. He meant to make himself a literary artist, and in Paris alone he could expect to find the technical practice of the literary arts. In Paris alone, a few men survived who talked their language, wrote prose, and constructed drama, as they modelled a statue or planned a structure.

Thus far, as commonly happens even to ambitious young men, the path was easy, and the outlook clear; but the illusion of ease and horizon seldom lasts long in Paris. A few days completely dispel it. Almost instantly the future becomes desperately difficult. Especially to an American, the processes and machinery of a French education are hard to apply in his home work. The French mind thinks differently and expresses its thought differently, so that the American, though he may actually think in French, will express his thought according to an American formula. Merely the language profits him little; the arts not much more; the history not at all; the poetry is ill suited to the genius of the English tongue; the drama alone is capable of direct application; in sum, it is the whole — the combination of tradition, mental habit, association of ideas, labor of technique, criticism, instinct — that makes a school, and the school, once mastered, is of only indirect use to an American. The secret of French literary art is a secret of its own which does not exist in America. Indeed, the American soon begins to doubt whether

America has any secrets, either in literary or any other art.

Within a few weeks all these doubts and difficulties had risen in young Lodge's face, and he found himself reduced to the usual helplessness of the art-student in Paris, working without definite purpose in several unrelated directions. At best, the atmosphere of Paris in December lacks gayety except for Parisians, or such as have made themselves by time and temperament, more or less Parisian. One flounders through it as one best can; but in Lodge's case, the strain was violently aggravated by the political storm suddenly roused by President Cleveland's Venezuela message, and sympathy with his father's political responsibilities in the Senate.

PARIS, *December 26, 1895.*

The study here is wholly different from anything I have been accustomed to and I am in some ways much alone. It seems to me here as if I was losing my grip, my aggressiveness, my force of mind, and it is a feeling that has been gradually coming over me, and that Venezuela has brought to a crisis. I don't do anything here, nothing tangible. I work five hours a day or six, and what on — a miserable little poetaster. I want to get home and get some place on a newspaper or anything of that kind, and really do something. I spend more money than is necessary, and altogether don't seem to lead a very profitable life. For me, loafing is not fun except in a recognized vacation. I never realized this until now. I thought I should like to take it easy for a while and *soi-disant* amuse myself. I am wretched. I want something real to do. I don't want to become a mere Teutonic grind, and it's necessary to do that if you are going to take degrees here. Both you and papa told me to feel no hesitation in coming home if I wanted to, and so now that I have been here long enough to see I have made an error, I write as I do. I am always slow of comprehension, and if it has taken me a long time to find this out, it's just that I am getting experience — rather slowly and stupidly. I have not yet absolutely decided. If this appears to you hasty or ill-advised, please let me know in the shortest way possible.

Venezuela excites me horribly and my poor mind is rather torn, as you may see by this somewhat incoherent letter.

Paris, *January 6, 1896.*

Since I last wrote you I have quieted down a good deal more. I feel as if I had been through three hideous weeks of madness and were become on a sudden sane. You see the Venezuela affair came on me on a sudden and filled me with such a longing for home that I lost all pleasure in things over here. So my poor mind whirled round and round from one thing to another till I almost went mad. Now Venezuela seems to be a danger only in the future if at all, and I am realizing how much I am getting here.

If papa is willing I should stay I can come back with a good knowledge of German, Italian and Spanish, and of Romance Philology and Middle Age Literature — all of which things I very much need.

The thing which tore me worst in all this mental struggle I have been going through was the continual thought of money and my crying inability to adapt myself to my time and to become a money-maker. I felt as if it was almost cowardly of me not to turn in and leave all the things I love and the world does n't, behind, and to adjust myself to my age, and try to take its ideals and live strongly and wholly in its spirit. It seems so useless being an eternal malcontent. Unless one is a Carlyle, to scream on paper generally ends in a thin squeak, and I fought and fought to try to be more a man of my age so that I might work with the tide and not against it. But it 's no use, I cannot stifle my own self or alter it in that way. I said to myself that I ought to go home in order to get into the tide of American life if for nothing else; that I ought n't to be dreaming and shrieking inside and poetizing and laboring on literature here in Paris, supported by my father, and that I ought to go home and live very hard making money. I said to myself that I knew I could not be very quick at money-making, but that at any rate in the eyes of men I should lead a self-respecting life and my hideous, utter failure would only be for myself and you, who understand. But somehow all the while my soul refused to believe the plain facts and illogically clung to the belief that I might do some good in creative work in the world after all, and so I struggled with the facts and my faiths and loves and there was the Devil of a row inside me and I most wretched. Now it seems to me that my staying here can do no harm, as I can just as well begin to be 19th century next year as this, and I shall have a very happy winter and acquire some knowledge and much experience. And so now my mind is comparatively calm and I am becoming happy again and seeing things a little more in their proper perspective.

Now like Marcus Aurelius I have come home to my own soul and found there, I am glad to say, sufficient strength and resource and calm to reëstablish my equilibrium, and make me see how cowardly it is not to have enough self-reliance to bear such things as these with a tolerably good grace. . . .

I might entitle this letter: "Of the entering, passing through, and coming out of, the madness of George Cabot Lodge." I really feel as if the past two weeks were a great black hole in my life, in which all my landmarks were blurred, and I have just found them again.

Paris, January 16, 1896.

I am now working principally on Romance Philology, Spanish and Italian. I usually go to the Bibliothèque in the morning and work on Spanish. I am studying the history of the literature and trying to read the most important things as I go along. It is hard work reading the old Spanish of the 12th to 15th centuries, but I am convinced it is the only way to know the language or literature really thoroughly. I also work on my Spanish courses. In Italian I am reading Tiraboschi, "Storia della litteratura Italiana," which of course is the great history of the Italian literature. I also work a good deal on Petrarch: he is one of my courses, you know. Mr. Stickney sent to Italy for me for a good edition of Dante, and when it comes I shall begin the study of it. In the afternoon I go to courses, and sometimes of course in the morning too, and play billiards as a rule about five with

Joe, and in the evening work on my Romance Philology. I have procured by good fortune a very good dictionary of the old French.

Thus, you see, my work now is concentrated on the Romance Languages and Literature, especially before the 16th century. I shall keep on principally on them, because I am sure by so doing I can come home with a more or less thorough knowledge of the Latin tongues and a little more than a smattering of their literature. The Latin languages attract me and I shall work hard on them. As for German, I shall learn it if I can find time, but I don't know. . . . I see now that I must do the best in me if I can; and if there is a best to do; and at any rate I have n't the force or the weakness to renounce everything without having one glorious fight for what I want to do and believe is best to do. It is this realization of my own self that has done me most good, I think.

I went to the Français last night. It was the birthday of Molière and they gave the "École des Femmes" and the "Malade Imaginaire," and afterwards the ceremony of crowning the bust by

all the *Sociétaires* and *pensionnaires* of the Théâtre.
It was most interesting. I think the best night of
theatre I ever had.

Paris, January 27, 1896.

My languages get on very well. Italian and
Spanish I am really getting very smart in and read
with perfect ease, and I am sure when I come back
I shall know a good deal about the Romance Languages. My German I am working on, and of
course it comes more slowly, but I think I can do it
all right.

Paris, February 21, 1896.

I have just lived through the Carnival here,
which began on Saturday night with the *bal de
l'opéra* (third of the name) and continued until
Wednesday morning. I took it in with considerable thoroughness. There was the procession of
the Bœuf Gras — the first time this has occurred
since the Franco-German war. It was very pretty
and the crowds in the street tremendous — all
throwing paper confetti and long rolls of paper,
which one might throw across the boulevards.

Now the trees are all covered with long ribbons of papers of all colors. It was a very pretty sight and most amusing. I never imagined such a good-tempered crowd, and one so bound to have a good time. I send by this mail a sort of programme with an amusing picture by Caran D'Ache. I was glad of the Carnival. I think one gets into terrible ruts and little habits close around one, and one gets dull and mechanical. The Carnival just broke all that up for me, and for three days I led a wholly irregular life, that had a certain splendor in the unexpectedness of everything I did. . . .

C. and P. both wrote me very nice things about my poems. I have just read over a lot and become drearily conscious that they are far from deserving any praise, so that it rather worries me to have people so kind about them, as it seems as if I could never live up to what they think I ought to do. However, I have become an excellent critic of my own work and diligently weed out from time to time all that seems flat, so that I may some day have something really poetry.

PARIS, *April 5*, 1896.

Here it's Easter Sunday and I have n't had a
happier day for a long time. The skies have been
bright blue and the sun pure gold, and the trees all
timidly "uttering leaves" everywhere, and so I
want to write to you. Early this morning Joe and I
went and rode horses in the Bois, which we had already done last Sunday, and are going to do more
often. It was most marvellous — all the little fresh
greening things looking out of the earth, and the
early sunlight coming wet and mild through the
trees, and the rare fresh air, and the sense of
physical glow and exercise.

I found an alley with about a dozen jumps in
it and whisked my old hired horse over the entire
lot, with the surprising result that he jumped
rather well, except the water-jump, into which
he flatly jumped, managing, however, to stand
up. Then I came home and read Petrarch and
Ronsard, and in the afternoon took a boat down
a bright blue Seine with white bridges spanning
it and a Louvre, etc., on either hand. I got off

at the Ile St. Louis, and for the pure dramatic
effect, went into the "Doric little morgue" and
saw two terrible dead old women with the lower
jaw dropped on the withered breast and the green
of decomposition beginning about the open eyes.
Then I came out into the broad sunshine, with
that blessed Cathedral Apse in front of me, and its
little sun-filled garden with the old Gothic fountain
running pure water, and felt it was very good to
live. Then I went in and heard a splendid mass,
with the great organ rolling up by the front rose-
window, and saw the Host raised and the church
full (really full) of people fall on their knees, and
the thick incense come slowly out, and felt alas!
how far away I was from the substance of the
shadow of splendor I was feeling. But I was very
happy for all that, and wandered around some
more in the sunlight, and then came home, where I
am now writing to you.

This winter I have been realizing a copy-book
commonplace, which is at the same time a metaphysical profundity, viz.: that the present is all

that *is* and it is not. One of the crowning metaphysical paradoxes. Of course the present is not.
While you are uttering "now," it is fled — it never
existed. It is like a geometrical point, non-ex-
istent. And the past — that's the cruel thing, the
killing memories. Memories of yesterday, of the
moment just fled, which are as hopelessly dead, as
impossibly distant as memories of ten years gone.
The past is like a great pit, and the present like a
frittered edge which is continually crumbling and
falling utterly down into the pit. . . . For me —
my past is all *amoncelé*, nothing nearer, nothing far-
ther. I have a more vivid memory of Sister with
long hair, driving old Rab up the side-walk by the
Gibsons' at Nahant on a gray autumn day, than
of most things happened within the year. And my
memories are all sad — sad with an infinite hopeless regret; that one of Sister for example has almost made me cry. And then the present is the
past so facilely, so quickly, and I find myself sometimes when I am not doing anything — talking
perhaps or sitting idle or even reading, in fact

un peu toujours, — suddenly turning sick and cold
and saying to myself, "See, your life goes, goes,
goes. Every day you get more memories to dwell
about you like mourning creatures, and still nothing done — with your youth, your strength, and
every minute the memories thickening and the
pain of them increasing, and still nothing done.
Man! Man! Your life is very short, already
twenty and two years; as many again, and you
will be hardened into your mould, and the mould
yet unmade! Up, up and do something!"

And the future — it is the veriest of common-
places to say the future does n't exist. It is nothing
but a probability — at best a hope. And then did
it ever occur to you that the present is like a piece
of paper on which experience writes in invisible ink,
and that only when the heat of the pain of memory
and regret blows upon it, do the characters come
out and you know how intensely alive, how happy,
or at any rate how miserable, or at least how un-
bored, you *had been.*

It seems to me all the happiness (except, of

course, physical) which we get is only the more or less incomplete suggestion or partial realization of some remembered happiness. For instance, the slant of the western sun through green leaves sometimes brings back one perfectly unimportant afternoon when I was very small, and Sister sat on the grass under those willows, behind the little toolhouse in front of Mr. Locke's, and read a story aloud to me.

She left off in the middle, and I can distinctly remember the last words she said. Now when I can get a vivid suggestion of something intensely happy in my memory, infinitely richer and more happy than I had any idea of when it occurred, it makes me more happy than anything. Happiness is a continual thinking backward or forward, memory or expectation.

This may all sound rather rhetorical, but I assure you it is unintentional. If you knew how intensely I have been feeling all this and much more that I cannot express, you would know that this is n't rhetoric, but pure crying out of the soul — such as I could only say to you.

Thousands of young people, of both sexes, pass through the same experience in their efforts to obtain education, in Paris or elsewhere, and are surprised to find at the end, that their education consists chiefly in whatever many-colored impressions they have accidentally or unconsciously absorbed. In these their stock or capital of experience is apt to consist, over and above such general training as is the common stock of modern society; but most of them would find themselves puzzled to say in what particular class of impression their gain was greatest. Lodge would have said at once that his gain was greatest in the friendship with young Stickney, to which the letters allude.

Joseph Trumbull Stickney, who was then preparing his thesis for the unusual distinction of doctorate at the Sorbonne, — the University of France, — was a European in the variety and extent of his education and the purest of Americans by blood, as his name proclaimed. Nearly of Lodge's age, almost identical in tastes and convictions, and looking forward to much the same career, he and his companionship were among those rare fortunes that sometimes bless unusually favored youth when it needs, more than all else, the constant contact with its kind.

CHAPTER III

"THE SONG OF THE WAVE"

EARLY in his college course, the young man had acquired a taste for Schopenhauer. The charm of Schopenhauer is due greatly to his clearness of thought and his excellence of style, — merits rare among German philosophers, — but another of his literary attractions is the strong bent of his thought towards Oriental and especially Buddhistic ideals and methods. At about the same time it happened that Sturgis Bigelow returned to Boston from a long residence in Japan, and brought with him an atmosphere of Buddhistic training and esoteric culture quite new to the realities of Boston and Cambridge. The mystical side of religion had vanished from the Boston mind, if it ever existed there, which could have been at best, only in a most attenuated form; and Boston was as fresh wax to new impressions. The oriental ideas were full of charm, and the oriental training was full

of promise. Young Lodge, tormented by the old
problems of philosophy and religion, felt the influence of Sturgis Bigelow deeply, for Bigelow was the
closest intimate of the family, and during the summer his island of Tuckanuck, near Nantucket, was
the favorite refuge and resource for the Lodges. As
time went on, more and more of the young man's
letters were addressed to Bigelow.

Returning home after the winter of 1895-96 in
Paris, he found himself more than ever harrowed
by the conflict of interests and tastes. He went
to Newport in August, for a few days, and rebelled
against all its standards. "I hate the philistine-
plutocrat atmosphere of this place, and it tends
not to diminish my views anent modern civilization and the money power. I sincerely thank God
I shall never be a rich man, and never will I, if
my strength holds. The world cannot be fought
with its own weapons; David fought Goliath with
a sling, and the only way to kill the world is to fight
it with one's own toy sword or sling, and deny.
strenuously contact with, or participation in, the
power it cherishes. Much more of the same nature

is yearning to be said, but I will spare you. . . . If I have n't it in me to write a poem, what a sordid farce my life will be!" The expression is strong, but in reality the young man had fairly reached the point where his life was staked on literary success. The bent of his energy was fixed beyond change, and as though he meant deliberately to make change impossible, he returned to Europe, to pass the next winter, 1896–97, in Berlin.

A winter in Berlin is, under the best of circumstances, a grave strain on the least pessimistic temper, but to a young poet of twenty-two, fresh from Paris, and exuberant with the full sense of life and health, Berlin required a conscientious sense of duty amounting to self-sacrifice, in order to make it endurable. Socially it was complete solitude except for the presence of Cecil Spring-Rice, an old Washington intimate then in the British Embassy. As a matter of education in art or literature, the study of German had never been thought essential to poets, or even to prose writers, in the English language; and although, at about the middle of the century, many of the best English and French authors, and some American, had insisted that no trained student could.afford to be ignorant of so important a branch of human effort, none had ever imposed it on their pupils as a standard of expression. In that respect, a serious devotion to the language was likely to do more harm than good.

The New England conscience is responsible for much that seems alien to the New England nature. Naturally, young Lodge would have gone to Rome to study his art, and no doubt he would have greatly preferred it. He needed to fill out his education on that side, — not on the side of Germany, —and his future work suffered for want of the experience. If he went to Berlin, he did it because in some vague way he hoped that Germany might lead to practical work. His letters show the strenuous conscientiousness with which he labored through the task.

TO HIS MOTHER

BERLIN, *January*, 1897.

It's a week now since I wrote you and I've not much more news than I had. I am very well off here. All German bedrooms are bad and mine no worse than the rest, I imagine — large enough for a bed and two tables for my books and papers, a porcelain stove and bureau, washstand, etc. To be sure, it has but one window, through which, by leaning uncomfortably to one side, one can perceive the withered corner of a gray garden, but otherwise facing a dirty wall of brick. But, as I say, it seems this is a chronic malady of German bedrooms, and besides I have the use of a very pleasant front room where I work in the morning, and afternoon, too, sometimes. The people here are very nice, and eager to make me comfortable; otherwise all my news is contained in the word work. Nearer ten hours than eight of this have I done every day — written translations from German, reading of German Grammar, reading Schiller with the man or his Frau, talking, going to the theatre, — "Faust," "The Winter's Tale," very good, and a translation of the "Dindon," etc. All German, you observe, and in fact it seemed best at first to let Greek and everything go, and devote every energy to the acquisition of this tongue —

infernally hard it is too. I found, right off, I didn't
know anything about it, and since then have really
made a good deal of progress.

It's wonderful how the soul clears itself up in
this sort of solitude in which I am living — picks
up all the ravelled threads and weaves them carefully together again, and gradually simplifies and
straightens itself out. All my life since last April
I have been going over, as I have some of my poems,
forcing the events into sequence and building a
sort of soul-history, fibrous and coherent. It's a
wonderful clearing out of refuse, and I feel strong
and self-reliant as I never did before. I have acquired the ability to write over poetry and work it
into shape, which is a great step forward, I believe,
and several of my poems have I been over in this
way with much advantage. And so I am almost
childlishly contented at getting back to an existence of sleep and food at a minimum and work at
a maximum, and I really think I have never
worked harder or lived more utterly simply. And
oh! It is good with the entire spiritual solitude
and mental solitude that I abide in.

BERLIN, *January* 17, 1897.

I am now, after infinite pains and vast expense, matriculate at the University here, with several large and most beautiful diplomas certifying in Latin that I am in fact matriculate. The diplomas alone are worth the price of admission. It was heavy, though — four solid mornings' work and about 75 marks. First I went with the man I am living with, and found I could n't hear any lectures at all unless I did matriculate and that to matriculate I had to have my degree from Cambridge, which I had carefully left at home. Then the next day I went to the Embassy and found Mr. Jackson, who had very kindly written me a letter already, saying he hoped I would come to see him when I wanted to. Well, Mr. Jackson gave me a letter certifying that I had a degree, and with this and my passport I went again to the University, and found I was too late that day and must come the next. So the next — this time alone — I went and passed — oh, such a morning! First I sat in a room while the Rector went over my papers; then I and two Germans were called in to the Rector

and he gave us handsome degrees and swore us to
obedience to all the rules of the University, and
then we shook hands with him. Then some one
said, "Go to room 4." So I and the two Germans
went, and there they wrote my name and birthplace and papa's business, which I tried to explain
and failed, and so he is registered in the Berlin
University as anything from a coal-heaver up.

All this time my nerves were rasping like taxed
wires for fear I should n't understand what was
said to me.

And then I wrote my own name, birthplace, etc.,
in my own sweet hand in another big book, and
then was given a little card where I wrote my name
again, and a huge card filled with questions. When
I understood them I answered; when not, I put
"ja" and "nein" alternately. Then they said,
"Go to room 15." So I went and gave a man my
filled-out card and he wrote something which he
gave me and said, "Go to room 4 zurück"; so I
went. There I got a book and another card, — the
last one, — and then I filled out all sorts of things
in the book and finally went to room 2, where I

paid out vast sums, got some receipts, and — left, a shattered man in mind and soul. The strain of trying to understand and write correctly and being always afraid you won't is really terrible. Then to-day I had to go again to see the Dean of the Philosophical Department in which I matriculated, and he gave me another beautiful degree. And now it's all over. I am an academischer Bürger, and if the police try to arrest me all I've got to do is to show my card and they can't touch me. . . .

This place is gray, gray, gray. I have done a constant stream of work, which has flowed in a steady and almost uninterrupted course, with six hours' sleep-interval in the twenty-four. I have been theatre-going a lot. I have seen a good deal of Shakespeare, Schiller, and Sudermann.

BERLIN, *January 26*, 1897.

It is for the best my being here, of that rest assured. I am entirely convinced that it was and is the very best thing possible for me in the circumstances, and I find sufficient content and interest, and especially work, to keep me far from stagnant.

As I wrote you, I feel a sense of increased strength and reliance, which I don't explain and don't try to. Sufficient that so it is. Much of my life have I overlooked and condemned and profited by in this solitude and I finally begin to feel a certain strength that I trust will urge into expression fit and simple and sufficient one day, and not be trampled under in this awful struggle to acquire a financial independence which I see is inevitable for me. Writing prose is the only utterly depressing thing I have done, and that, D. V., I shall learn by mere gritting of teeth.

I've this moment got back from Dresden, where I've been since Friday with Springy [1] — a little vacation. It's very pretty and the gallery very wonderful. Naturally there I spent my days, and twice I went to the opera.

BERLIN, *February 9*, 1897.

I have written some new verse and written over with much time and labor a good deal more old. It's with the greatest difficulty that I can take any

[1] Cecil Spring-Rice.

other form of literary endeavor seriously; and put
my heart in it, I can't. I live and breathe in an
atmosphere of imagination and verse here, all alone
when I am not a working-machine, and it's all
around me like a garment. It's hard to express
what I mean — but the other day I went early to
the University and saw a radiant sunrise through
the snowy Thiergarten and sort of sang inside all
the rest of the day — odd rhythms with here and
there a word. I was so content I did n't even want
to write down anything. I wonder if you have ever
had the feeling — I suppose you have — of having
a beautiful thing compose the scatteredness of
your mind into an order, a rhythm, so that you
think and feel everything rhythmically. My expression is weak, but if you've had it you'll know
what I mean.

I saw the whole of "Wallenstein" the other
day — or rather in two successive evenings —
first the "Lager" and the "Picolomini," and second evening the "Tod," which is certainly very
fine — both dramatically and poetically, — quite
the biggest German play I've seen. I'm reading

"Faust" with my teacher here, and admiring very much of it.

I have been reading over some of Schopenhauer and Kant in the German and enjoying it immensely. I think the study and pursuit of pure metaphysical thought makes a man more contentedly, peacefully happy than any other thing. There is a white purity consisting in its utter lack of connection to the particular, in its entire devotion to the pure, synthetical ideas which never touch the feeling, individual world, which makes metaphysics the nearest approach to will-lessness, to pure intellectual contemplation, that I know. And of course, as all suffering is willful (in its essential meaning) and emotional, pure intellectual contemplation must be that privation of suffering in which happiness consists — for I become more than ever convinced that in this world of evil and separation happiness is only the privation of pain as good is the privation of evil. 'Tis only the transcendent emotion that you get in poetry or in great passions such as pity and love, that can be called positive happiness. Pity or love, I mean, so aggrandized that the sense of individuality is lost in the feeling of union with the whole where there is no space or time or separation. That is, that only morally and esthetically can one be positively happy — all other happiness must be simply the denial of pain. Metaphysics is the completest expression of such a denial, I think, and also with an almost esthetic poetic value some times — in some metaphysicians an undoubted poetic value, as for instance in Plato and Schopenhauer. But it seems I am writing you an essay on metaphysics, so I will stop.

BERLIN, *February, late,* 1897.

I am gradually digging a way into the language, and you'd be suprised at my fluent inaccuracy in the German tongue, and I can write it pretty well, too. Reading is thoroughly acquired, and I am more than satisfied with my progress. I have heard a good deal of music which always does me good, though, as Joe tells me, I don't in the least understand it. I saw the Emperor the other day for the first time, and rather a fine strong face he has.

I really believe that nothing I ever did benefited me as much as has this short time here. I have grown more rigid and surer of myself, and withal have acquired a certain capacity and love of a great deal of work, which I never had before, and which is only surpassed by my love of not doing work after I have done a great deal. My poetry, I think, shows that — I have tried to hope so. Please tell me if you think any of the things I sent you show a clearer, firmer touch than before. As I say, I try to think so and almost feel sometimes as if it really was in me after all to speak a strong sincere word clearly for men to hear; but then, on the other hand, whiles I think I am going to dry up, and in my perfectly lucid moments, I see with a ghostly distinctness how far short all my work falls of what I seem sometimes to know as an ideal.

The dear Springy came to see me yesterday and I had a good talk with him and subsequently dined with him. I've seen very little of him this month, as society has been on the rampage, and he has rampaged with it perforce. He went to London for a week to-day, but when he comes back, the

world will be quiet and I expect to see a great
deal of him.

The German experience added little or nothing
to his artistic education, for Schopenhauer can be
studied anywhere, and neither Goethe nor Schiller
needs to be read in Berlin; but his letters show that
his enforced, solitary labor during this winter threw
him back upon himself, and led him to publish his
work before he fairly knew in what direction his
strength lay. During these three years of post-grad-
uate education he had toiled, with sure instinct, to
learn the use of his tools, and chiefly of his tongue.
All art-students must go through this labor, and
probably the reason why so many young poets
begin by writing sonnets is that the sonnet is the
mode of expression best adapted for practice; it
insists on high perfection in form; any defect or
weakness betrays itself, and the eye can cover fourteen lines at once without too great an effort. Lodge
liked the labor of sonnet-writing, and it taught him
the intricacies of language and the refinements of
expression which every literary artist must try at

least to understand, even when he does not choose
to practise them; but, at heart, Lodge was less a
poet than a dramatist, though he did not yet know
it; and the dramatic art is the highest and most ex-
acting in all literature. The crown of genius belongs
only to the very rare poets who have written
successful plays. They alone win the blue ribbon
of literature. This was the prize to which Lodge,
perhaps unconsciously, aspired, and his labor in
sonnet-writing, however useful as training in verse,
was no great advantage for his real purpose, even
though he had Shakespeare for his model.

On the other hand, the lack of society in a manner compels the artist to publish before he is ready.
The artist, living in a vacuum without connection
with free air, is forced by mere want of breath to
cry out against the solitude that stifles him; and
the louder he cries, the better is his chance of
attracting notice. The public resents the outcry,
but remembers the name. A few — very few —
readers appreciate the work, if it is good, on its
merits; but the poet himself gets little satisfaction from it, and, ten years afterwards, will pro-

bably think of it only as a premature effort of his youth.

To this rule a few exceptions exist, like Swinburne's "Poems and Ballads," where the poet, at the first breath, struck a note so strong and so new as to overpower protest; but, as a rule, recognition is slow, and the torpor of the public serves only to discourage the artist, who would have saved his strength and energy had he waited. When young Lodge returned from Germany in the summer of 1897, he felt himself unpleasantly placed between these two needs,—that of justifying his existence, on the one hand, and that of challenging premature recognition, on the other. He chose boldly to assert his claims to literary rank, and justified his challenge by publishing, in the spring of 1898, the volume of a hundred and thirty-five pages, called "The Song of the Wave."

Here are some eighty short poems, one half of which are sonnets, and all of which reflect the long tentative, formative effort of the past five years. Most of them have a personal character, like "The Song of the Wave" itself, which has been already quoted. From a simple, vigorous nature like Lodge's, one would have expected, in a first effort, some vehement or even violent outburst of self-assertion; some extravagance, or some furious protest against the age he lived in; but such an attitude is hardly more than indicated by the dedication to Leopardi. The exordium, "Speak, said my soul!" expresses rather his own need of strength and the solitude of his ambitions: —

> Speak! thou art lonely in thy chilly mind,
> With all this desperate solitude of wind,
> The solitude of tears that make thee blind, ¡
>   Of wild and causeless tears.
> Speak! thou hast need of me, heart, hand and head,
> Speak, if it be an echo of thy dread,
> A dirge of hope, of young illusions dead, —
>   Perchance God hears!

Most of these poems are echoes of early youth, of the ocean, of nature: simple and vigorous expressions of physical force, with an occasional recurrence to Schopenhauer and Leopardi; but the verses that most concern the artist are those which show his effort for mastery of his art, and his progress in power of expression. He scattered such

verses here and there, for their own sake, on nearly
every page, as most young poets do, or try to do,
and such verses are more or less a measure, not only
of his correctness of ear, but of his patient labor.
Take, for instance, the first half-dozen lines of
"The Gates of Life," which happens to be written
in a familiar metre: —

Held in the bosom of night, large to the limits of wonder,
Close where the refluent seas wrinkle the wandering sands,
Where, with a tenderness torn from the secrets of sorrow, and
    under
The pale pure spaces of night felt like ineffable hands,
The weak strange pressure of winds moved with the moving of
    waters,
Vast with their solitude, sad with their silences, strange with
    their sound,
Comes like a sigh from the sleep . . .

This metre seems to call for excessive elabora-
tion of phrase; a few pages further, the poet has
tried another metre which repels all such refinements; it is called "Age," and begins: —

    Art thou not cold?
    Brother, alone to-night on God's great earth?

The two last stanzas run: —

Shalt thou not die,
Brother ? the chill is fearful on thy life,
Shalt thou not die ?
Is this a lie ?
This threadbare hope — of death ?
A lie, like God, and human love, and strife
For pride, and fame, — this soiled and withered wreath.

Art thou not cold ?
Brother ? alone on God's great earth to-night;
Art thou not cold ?
Art thou not old
And dying and forlorn ?
Art thou not choking in the last stern fight
While in divine indifference glows the morn ?"

The sonnet, again, offers a different temptation.
The verses tend of their own accord to group themselves about the favorite verse. The first sonnet in
this series begins with what Mrs. Wharton calls
the magnificent apostrophe to Silence: —

Lord of the deserts, 'twixt a million spheres, —

and need go no further; the rest of the lines infalli-
bly group themselves to sustain the level of the
first. So, the sonnet to his own Essex begins with
the singularly happy line, —

Thy hills are kneeling in the tardy spring, —

which leads to an echo in the last verse: —

We know how wanton and how little worth
Are all the passions of our bleeding heart
That vex the awful patience of the earth.

The sonnet to his friend Stickney after reading the twelfth-century Roman of "Amis and Amile," begins: —

And were they friends as thou and I are friends, —

in order to work out the personal touch of their common ambition: —

Ah, they who walked the sunshine of the world,
And heard grave angels speaking through a dream,
Had never their unlaurelled brows defiled,
Nor strove to stem the world's enormous stream.

The form of the sonnet tends to carry such verbal or personal refinements to excess; they become labored; perhaps particularly so in denunciation, like the sonnet, "Aux Modernes," which begins: —

Only an empty platitude for God;

and ends with the line, —

The hard, gray, tacit distances of dawn.

Such work marks the steps of study and attainment rather than attainment itself, as the second "Nirvana" marks effort: —

TO W. STURGIS BIGELOW

December 10, 1897.

I will trouble you with this poem, which here I send to you. I wrote it without correction in half an hour before dinner, and I feel of it, as I have felt of so many of my things, that no one will understand it except you; also I know it's my fault and not theirs that no one will understand it — my implements are still so rude — my ideas seem luminous and limpid while they are wordless, and, I think, owing to practice, most ideas come to me now wordless — but in words they become crude, misty, and imperfect; whiles I feel quite hopeless. But you have been there, have seen vividly all I've half perceived and you can supply my lapses in coherency. This was, I think, the result of an hour's practice last night. Certainly if it has a merit, it is that I have not been economical in this poem, every word seems to me now over-full with

meaning. My soul has gone into the writing of it
and, good Lord, it's melancholy to feel how it
might have been said — luminously and unavoid-
ably — and how it is said — Well! perhaps, some
day! . . . if I could only be with you to try to tell
you all I have endeavored to say in these fourteen
lines!

NIRVANA

Woof of the scenic sense, large monotone
  Where life's diverse inceptions, Death and Birth,
  Where all the gaudy overflow of Earth
  Die — they the manifold, and thou the one.
Increate, complete, when the stars are gone
  In cinders down the void, when yesterday
  No longer spurs desire starvation-gray,
  When God grows mortal in men's hearts of stone;
As each pulsation of the heart divine
  Peoples the chaos, or with falling breath
  Beggars creation, still the soul is thine!
And still, untortured by the world's increase,
  Thy wide harmonic silences of death,
  And last — thy white, uncovered breast of peace!

I will now, as did Michael Angelo, add a com-
mentary: —

Nirvana is the woof on which sense traces its

scenic patterns; it is the one, the monotone upon which death and birth, both inceptions, in that death is merely the beginning of changed conditions of life, and "the gaudy overflow of earth"— that is, all finite things and emotions — sing their perishable songs and, as rockets disperse their million sparks which die on the universal night-blackness, so they die and leave the constant unchanging monotone. Nirvana is in-create because never created, and of course complete. Yesterday spurs desire to a state of starvation-grayness because desire and hope look back on every yesterday as a renewed disappointment. The phrase meant life. "When God grows mortal in men's hearts of stone," has two meanings, first that when men grow unbelieving God perishes — God being the creature of belief; and second that Nirvana endureth when God himself perishes. The next three lines are an embodiment of the idea that with every beat of the heart divine a cosmos swells into existence, and with every subsiding of this heart it sinks, perishes into nothingness. Also from line five to line eleven means that after everything and through everything the soul is still Nirvana's, if I can so express myself; thus reiterating the idea suggested in the first quatrain, that the condition of the finite is separateness and of the spiritual, unity; and that all life, though clothed in diverse forms, holds in it the identical soul which is Nirvana's, attained or potential. The world's increase is of course the cycle of life and death in its largest sense. This is of course a mere shadowing forth of the ideas I had in writing the poem. You will see their possible amplifications.

January, 1898.

Poetry is an absolute necessity for me, but when I think of dumping a volume of verse that nobody will read on to a gorged world, I say to myself: "*A quoi bon?*" The foolish publisher will have to be found first, however, so I don't worry. Does the enclosed ("The Wind of Twilight — Tuckanuck") say anything to you? The long things (Oh, be thankful) are too long to send, so I send this. I've done several of these sorts of things lately.

To the cold critic, this stage of an artist's life is the most sympathetic, and the one over which he would most gladly linger. He loves the youthful freshness, the candor, the honest workmanship, the naïf self-abandonment of the artist, in proportion as he is weary of the air of attainment, of cleverness, of certainty and completion. He would, for his own amusement, go on quoting verse after verse to show how the artist approaches each problem of his art, what he gains; what he sacrifices; but this is the alphabet of criticism, and can be practised on Eginetan marbles or early Rembrandts better than on youthful lyrics. The interested reader has only to read for himself.

CHAPTER IV

WAR AND LOVE

In January, 1898, young Lodge was in Washington, acting as secretary to his father, varying between office-work all day and composition the greater part of the night. The outbreak of the Spanish War drew him at once into the government service, and he obtained a position as cadet on board his uncle Captain Davis's ship, the Dixie. During the three summer months that this war in the tropics lasted, he had other things than poems to think about, and his letters convey an idea that perhaps the life of naval officer actually suited his inherited instincts best.

TO HIS MOTHER

FORTRESS MONROE, *May*, 1898.

Here I am and here I rest until Saturday, when the ship will probably sail. I am, and feel like, a perfect fool. Everybody knows everything and I don't know anything; but they are kind and I guess I shall get on when the thing gets fairly started. I went over and saw the ship to-day and she is fine — at any rate while I am here in this business, I am going to learn all I can.

NEWPORT NEWS, *May 20*, 1898.

I am getting on as well as possible and learning a good deal all the time. There is plenty of room for learning. These great golden days go over me, and it seems as if all the real imaginative side of me was under lock and key. The practical things occupy me entirely.

FORTRESS MONROE, *June 2*, 1898.

We have been taking on coal all day, and before it's all aboard we shall be chock-full. Uncle Harry has got orders to be ready to sail at a moment's notice, and he is going to telegraph to-night that he is all ready. I hope it may mean that we are to be moved out of here very soon toward the scene of action. A day or two ago we went out for thirty-six hours and fired all the big guns. I fired both mine myself, and was surprised to find the shock not at all serious. The whole process was very interesting, and I shall try to remember it all and be able to tell you all about it when I get back. I get on pretty well. There is one thing I am convinced of and that is that I can make my gun-crews fight and my guns effective, and that is after all the principal thing.

The internal condition of Spain makes me believe that the war must end soon. I only hope it will last long enough to insure our possession of Cuba, Porto Rico, and the Philippines, and give me one fight for my money.

OFF CIENFUEGOS, CUBA, *June 25*, 1898.

We reached the squadron the day after I wrote from Mole St. Nicolas, and were immediately sent down here to patrol. In fact, the Admiral gave Uncle Harry discretion to do pretty much what he pleased. We came down and on our way destroyed two block-houses which were at the southern end of the Trocha. The next day we engaged a battery at a place called Trinidad, and yesterday we engaged the same battery, a gun-

boat in the harbor, and a gun-boat that came out
at us, and used them up pretty badly. So you see
I am in it. Nothing very serious so far, but still we
have been under fire and have killed a good many
Spaniards. It is a most beautiful coast all along
here, great splendid hills close to the water's edge,
and splendid vegetation. The weather has been
hot, but very fine and to me excessively pleasant,
and I am quite happy to be on the scene of action
and in the way of seeing all that's going. My two
guns have behaved very well and I have had several very nice compliments from the First Lieutenant. We relieved the Yankee here and she
goes to-day to Key West for coal, which gives me
a chance to send this letter. I really enjoy the life
immensely, far more than I thought I should —
the work interests me, and I am learning a good
deal every day. Last night Uncle Harry and I
dined with Captain Brownson on the Yankee and
it was very interesting.

August, 1898.

Many thanks for your letter which I have just
got to-day. I am more than delighted we are going

to Spain. We came up from Cape Cruz on the 6th
and saw the wrecks of the Spanish fleet lying up on
the beach below Santiago — a great sight. It's a
great business to be here and see the wheels go
round and be a wheel one's self, even if not a very
big one. I am very glad on the whole I came as a
cadet and not as an ensign, for as a cadet I am not
supposed to know anything, which puts me in a
true position and not a false one. None of these
militia officers know any more than I do, and they
are in false positions. Anyway, I do a lot of work
and I think accomplish something. It hardly
seems as if the war could last now, and I only
hope it will hang on long enough to give us a
whack at Camara and the Spanish coast.

Yesterday we got the first ice we have had since
June 15, and to-day the first mail since we left Old
Point.

U. S. S. Dixie, *August 5*, 1898.

We left Guantanamo after having coaled, and
went to Puerto Rico with the troops. On the way
we were detached from the convoy and sent all
round the island to hunt up transports, and so we

did not get to Guanica until after the army had landed. We got there in the morning, and that afternoon we were sent with the Annapolis and the Wasp — Uncle Harry [1] being the senior officer — down to Ponce, Puerto Rico. We got there about four and went peacefully into the harbor. Then Uncle Harry sent Mr. Merriam [2] in to demand the surrender of the place, and I went along. We landed under a flag of truce, and found that there was a Spanish Colonel with about 300 men, who said he would "die at his post." He was back in the town, which is about two miles inland. However, during the night delegates came off and surrendered the town, on condition that the troops be allowed to withdraw, which we granted, and at six o'clock the next morning, we went in again and I myself raised the flag over the office of the Captain of the Port, amid immense enthusiasm of the populace. Haines,[3] the marine officer, was put in charge with a file of marines, and put guards and sentries

[1] Captain Davis, commanding the Dixie.
[2] Lieutenant and executive officer of the Dixie.
[3] Lieutenant of Marines on the Dixie.

on the Customs House and other public places; and
then two other officers and I got into a carriage,
with a Puerto Rican friend, and drove up to the
town.

It was most picturesque. The town had been
deserted fearing a bombardment, and from every
nook and corner crowds appeared cheering and
crying, "Viva los conquistadores Americanos";
"Viva el Puerto Rico libre." We drove through the
town, the crowd and enthusiasm increasing always,
and finally returned and got Haines, who had formally delivered the town to General Miles when he
landed. . . . We then went back to Ponce with
Haines. We were taken to the club and to the
headquarters of the fire-brigade — everywhere
amid yelling mobs. While we were there I heard
that there were some political prisoners confined
in the City Hall. I told Haines, who was senior
officer, and he went over to see about liberating
them.

Ponce is the largest town in Puerto Rico, about
40,000 people. The City Hall stands at one end of
a great square — about as large as Lafayette

Square. In it is the Mayor's office and the court-room, with a dais and throne where the judges sat. There Haines liberated sixteen political prisoners; for the army, though supposed to be in possession of the town, had not taken the City Hall. Finding this to be the case, I got an American flag and told Haines I was going to raise it over the City Hall. I then went onto the roof where the flag-staff was, taking with me the Mayor of Ponce. There with great solemnity, the Mayor and I bare-headed, I raised the flag. The whole square was swaying with people, and as the flag went up they cheered — such a noise as I never heard. Then the Mayor and I went below and the Mayor presented me with his staff of office, the Spanish flag which flew over the City Hall, and the banner of Ponce, and formally delivered over to me his authority. I sent to the barracks where were our soldiers, and got some over to occupy the City Hall. I then, with great ceremony, gave back to the Mayor his badge of office and the town of Ponce. Shortly after we left.

GUANTANAMO BAY, CUBA, *August* 10, 1898.

I got your letter just a day or two ago, and mighty glad I was to get it. The flagship has just signalled "Associated Press dispatch states that peace protocol has been arranged." I suppose this is the end. If so, if hostilities cease and peace is eventually certain, I wish you would find out if the Dixie is to be put out of commission. I suppose it will take three or four months to patch up the treaty and have it ratified, and if the Dixie is to lie here or convoy transports during that time, I should like very much to be detached and ordered home on waiting orders, until my resignation is sent in and accepted. I suppose there would be no trouble about this. I came for the war, and as this isn't and never will be my life when the war is over, I want to get home as soon as possible, and pick up life again where I left off. Of course if the Dixie is to be put right out of commission, I should much prefer to go out of active service with the ship, and I should think that the Department would not wish to keep these auxiliary ships, manned with militia, in service any longer than was absolutely

necessary. Well, I have learned a good deal and I
am mighty glad I came. I have n't seen as much
fighting as some, but I have had my share of the
fun, I think, and anyway one does one's best and
takes the chances of war. I really think I have
made myself useful, and at least have not encum-
bered or hurt the service by coming, and that's as
much as an amateur can hope for. Anyway I've
worked hard. I shall have a great story to tell you
about Ponce, of which "Magna pars fui," and I
have got some splendid trophies. I have had a
good time and am happy now; but as peace grows
more certain I long to get home and see you all
again. It seems an enormous stretch of time since
I left you.

Extract from a letter of CAPTAIN DAVIS to H. C. L.

July 20, 1898.

. . . He [G. C. L.] shows unbounded zeal and
unflagging industry, and a great aptitude for the
profession. He has already developed the real
sailor's trick of being always the first on hand. No
one has ever been known to say, "Where is Mr.

Lodge?" This is not the encomium of a fond uncle.
I see very little of him on duty except in working
ship, when his station is near mine. He is a daily
companion to me in hours of leisure, but on duty
he is the First Lieutenant's man, and I notice he is
always called on for duty where promptness and
intelligence are required. I could give you a much
higher estimate of his usefulness if I quoted Merriam, than in recording my own observation.

Brought back again to the chronic divergence
between paths of life, the young man struggled as
he best could to assert his mastery over his own
fate, and developed a persistence of will that
amounted to primitive instinct rather than to reasoning process. Constantly he threw himself with
all his energy in the direction which led away
from the regular paths of modern activity. He was
familiar with them all, if only as Secretary of a
Senate Committee, and he read science quite as
seriously as poetry, but when he came to action he
always widened the gap between himself and his
world. "The Song of the Wave" was his first

public act of divorce. Only the difficulty of finding a publisher prevented him from taking a tone
much more hostile to society, in novels, which he
wrote and burned one after another, because they
failed to satisfy him. His letters to his early friend,
Marjorie Nott, have much to say of this phase
of mind. On September 12, 1899, he wrote from
Tuckanuck : —

TO MISS MARJORIE NOTT

Why do your letters make me so needlessly
happy! I think it's because you believe in so much
and because I do too, and need to have some one
to tell me that it is so. Not that I doubt, — what
would my life be if I doubted! No, it's only that
pretty much everybody believes I'm a crank or a
fool, or asks when I'm going to begin to do something; — to which question, by the way, I invariably respond—never! and oh! it's so good not to
be on the defensive, not to feel the good anger
rising in you, and step on it because you know they
won't understand; not to suffer with the desire to
insult the whole world; to lay its ugliness naked;

to say: "There, there! don't you see all the dust
and ashes that we're all admiring? don't you
see? don't you understand?" And then not say it,
because you know they can't see, and they won't
understand. Ah, yes! it's so good to sit here, and
write all this rot to you, and think that you'll
know, that you'll understand. Is n't it horrible to
get your mind twisted into cheap cynicisms while
the tears are falling in your heart? and it's what we
have to do, — nous autres! I shall certainly end
in publishing my book if I can find a bold enough
publisher. The temptation is too immense. I know
they won't understand, and yet I'm young enough
to hope they will. Do you remember the book I
talked to you of last winter? Well, that's it! I've
done it over again, and — well! I don't know! I
don't know why I write all this. I am here so calm,
with my brother the sun and my sister the sea, —
by the way, Tuckanuck, — and I feel as if I was
anywhere except in the hither end of the nineteenth century; and my book, I don't think of it
at all here. I write verse now — nothing else.

Naturally, since man or bird began to sing, he has sung to the woman, — or the female. The male is seldom a sympathetic listener; he prefers to do his own singing, or not to sing at all. He is not much to blame, but his indifference commonly ends by stifling the song, and the male singer has to turn to the female, or perish. In America, the male is not only a bad listener, but also, for poetry, a distinctly hostile audience; he thinks poorly of poetry and poets, so that the singer has no choice but to appeal to the woman. That young Lodge should have done so with an intensity proportioned to the repression of his instinct for sympathy and encouragement elsewhere, was inevitable. Poets have always done it, but they have not shown by any means the surest instinct of poetry in their affairs of love, so that perhaps a woman who should criticise their work might feel tempted to use this test as the surest proof of force or failure in their instinct for art. By such a test, young Lodge would take rank among the strongest. Little credit is due to any man for yielding to altogether extraordinary beauty and charm in the perfection of feminine ideals, — although few men do it, — but it is far from being a rule that young men who rebel against the world's standards, and with infinite effort set up a standard of private war on the world, and maintain it with long and exhausting endurance, should go directly into the heart of the society they are denouncing, and carry off a woman whom lovers less sensitive to beauty, and less youthful in temperament, than poets or artists, might be excused for adoring.

Elizabeth Davis — another survival of rare American stock: Davis of Plymouth, Frelinghuysen of New Jersey, Griswold of Connecticut, with the usual leash of Senators, Cabinet officers, and other such ornaments, in her ancestry — was in truth altogether the highest flight of young Lodge's poetry, as he constantly told her when her own self-confidence naturally hesitated to believe it; and since his letters to her strike a note which rises high above the level of art or education, they cannot be wholly left out of his life. The man or woman who claims to be a poet at all, must prove poetry to the heart, and neither Shakespeare nor

Shelley can be exempted from the proof, — neither Dante nor Petrarch, — whatever their society might think about it.

Lodge's letters began in March, 1899, when he was starting with his father and mother on a trip to Europe, which led to Sicily. From New York he wrote to bid good-bye; the engagement was not yet avowed. And from Rome, a month later: —

TO MISS DAVIS

I saw the grave of Keats the other day, and also of Shelley. It was a very keen sensation — more living, I think, than anything I have felt since you. My life is happy here, but my soul is very dolorous and strenuous. In life nothing resolves itself well. If a good issue is to come to anything, so much must be struggled with and sacrificed, so much confusion and distress, before serenity comes! When one is very young, it does n't seem fitting. One wants so much! Heaven and Earth is hardly enough for the large desire of youth, and the gates of possible expansion close one by one, until at last one runs through the last one just closing, without

perhaps its being the right one. The period of
choice is very short; then comes the short, sharp
stab of necessity, and then — one has made one's
bed, and one must lie in it. It's all very eager and
restless, and perhaps better for being so.

From Rome in April he wrote: —

"One makes oneself so very largely, and to
make oneself greater or better, one must believe.
Apply your religion: "Thy faith has made thee
whole!" That's the most wonderful thing Christ
ever said, and it applies everywhere in life. Believe in yourself! it should be so easy for you. I
do it, and it is of course far harder for me, for
I've less to believe in.

The young people had much need to believe in
themselves, for, in a worldly point of view, they
had not much else to believe in. He wrote in July:

TO HIS MOTHER

BOSTON, *July,* 1899.

I am almost crazed with the desire to be independent, and yet I won't do anything that I don't

approve and I won't give up my writing, God willing. I must keep at it and accomplish what I can in
my own way. I feel sure it's the only way for me,
and I know my intention is not low, whatever my
performance may be. I feel desperate sometimes
that it all comes so slowly and that I do no better;
but I grit my teeth and keep at it. The agony
of getting a thought into adequate expression is
enormous. However, I feel so much resolution
that I take heart, and now, too, I see my path
clearer ahead of me. I must write and write, and
as I say, I believe my purposes are good.

TUCKANUCK, *September*, 1899.

I have n't written for a long time, I am afraid,
but since I have been here — the last ten days — I
have been so happy in the sun and sea that I
have n't written to any one at all and have hardly
done any work. I have just lived very happily. I
have begun to write a tragedy in verse, and it's
terrible work and not very encouraging. However,
I get along — I have in my head also a plot for a
prose play, very good, I think, and some other

things besides. Indeed my mind is quite fertile, and physically I am in splendid condition. I got a letter from Mr. Stedman this morning, who is preparing an anthology of American poets and wants to put me in it. J'apporte un bagage assez mince, but still if he can find anything he wants to print he is welcome to it.

A few days afterwards, he wrote from Boston:—

TO MISS DAVIS

To get away, very far from all this greasy gossip, this world of little motives and little desires! We must do it very soon. Only men who live in the constant strain of feeling alone against the world are forced to concentrate their passions on an object that seems to them above the world.

CHAPTER V

MARRIAGE

NATURALLY, life cannot be lived in heroics. The man who places himself out of line with the current of society sees most the ridiculous or grotesque features of his surroundings, and finds most in them to laugh at. The conviction that either he or society is insane,— or perhaps, both, — becomes a fixed idea, with many humorous sides; and though the humor tends to irony and somewhat cruel satire, it is often genial and sometimes playful. Young Lodge laughed with the rest, at the world or himself by turns. When Bigelow rebelled at his anarchic handwriting, he replied: —

TO W. STURGIS BIGELOW

Ballade d'ung excellent poëte au Sieur Bigelow au sujet d'ung certain plaint dudit Sieur Bigelow a luy addressé.

BALLADE

I

I like to see the phrases flow
   So smooth in writing round and plain —
Pooh! Hang the time and trouble! Though
   It gave me fever on the brain

And caused intolerable pain
In hand and wrist — you set at nought
    The beautiful, and still maintain
That writing must be slave to thought.

II

I wrote for beauty and I know
    That beauty is its own best gain;
"Art for art's sake," I cried, and so
    My unintelligible train
    Of words was writ — you grew insane
Trying to read them, for you sought
    A meaning and you swore again
That writing must be slave to thought.

III

You held the sheet above, below
    Your head, and every nerve did strain
To read, and from your lips did go
    Grim curses manifold as rain.
    You should have known your toil was vain;
For Art's sole sake my writing wrought;
    I scorned the axiom with disdain
That writing must be slave to thought.

IV

Prince, speak! Does anything remain
    Now art is gone? No sense you've caught!
Then tell not me, the pure inane,
    That writing must be slave to thought.

Fin de la Ballade d'ung excellent poëte au Sieur Bigelow. Composée et mise en escript ce neuvième Décembre A. D. MDCCCXCIX.

From Washington, on April 28, he wrote again
to Bigelow:—

Well! the point is here! one should learn that
it is not life that should be taken seriously, but living. In that way, one gets pleasure if not happiness. I wish I was going to Tuckanuck with you
right off; but I'm not, and I have yards and miles
of drudgery that maketh the heart sick. I've got
to write another play before June. I have written
several this winter, all on a steadily decreasing
scale of merit, and I hope this one will be bad
enough to be successful. The trees are full of
leaves, and the air full of sun, and only I am vile.
I wish I could pretend it was all somebody else's
fault, but I can't. *Voilà!*

A successful play needs not only to be fairly bad
in a literary sense, but bad in a peculiar way which
had no relation with any standard of badness that
Lodge could reach. He toiled in vain.

When one is twenty-six years old, splendid in
health and strength, and still more splendid in

love, one enjoys the exuberant energy of complaint
with a Gargantuan appetite:—

WASHINGTON, *May* 16, 1900.

Here it has been as high as 106° — Why don't
you go to Tuckanuck? I would if I could, Gawd
knows. It is of course self-evident to you as it is to
me, that in the event of one's absence the world
will cease to function, — but then who the Devil
cares whether it functions or not? Not you, nor yet
I. I would willingly barter the tattered remnants
of a devilish tried soul to be under one of the great
waves on the outside beach and, please Heaven, I
soon shall be doing it. Meanwhile I grovel along
in the living heat which I like, and do all the work
that's in me — but after these months of it, the
supply is running a little short, I'm afraid. I suppose I am here for about three weeks more — and
then, with your permission, kind Sir! surf, Sir! and
sun, Sir! and nakedness! — Oh, Lord! how I want
to get my clothes off — alone in natural solitudes.
In this heavy springtime I grow to feel exquisitely

pagan, and worship the implacable Aphrodite, and read Sappho (with considerable difficulty) in the Greek.

From the beginnings of life, the poet and artist have gone on, surprising themselves always afresh by the discovery that their highest flights of poetry and art end in some simple and primitive emotion; but the credit of seeing and feeling it is the best proof of the poet. In his next volume of Poems, published in 1902, two years afterwards, he put these emotions into verse, — "for E. L.," — no longer Elizabeth Davis but Elizabeth Lodge.

She moves in the dusk of my mind, like a bell with the sweet-
    ness of singing
In a twilight of summer fulfilled with the joy of the sadness of
    tears;
And the calm of her face, and the splendid, slow smile are as
    memories clinging
Of songs and of silences filling the distance of passionate years.

She moves in the twilight of life like a prayer in a heart that is
    grieving,
And her youth is essential and old as the spring and the fresh-
    ness of spring;

And her eyes watch the world and the little low ways of the
    sons of the living,
As the seraph might watch from the golden grave height of his
    heaven-spread wing.

The variations on this oldest of themes are endless, and yet are eternally new to some one who dis-
covers them afresh; so that very slight differences
of expression have artistic value. So, for example,
the sonnet beginning: —

    Why are you gone? I grope to find your hand.
    Why are you gone? The large winds seaward-bound,
    Tell of long journeying in the endless void.
    Why are you gone? I strain to catch the sound
    Of footsteps, watch to see the dark destroyed
    Before your lustrous fingers that would creep
    Over my eyes, and give me strength to sleep.

One does not venture to suggest a famous line of
a great poet for the sake of imitating the art, but
one does it readily for the sake of rivalling the
feeling. "You and I have gone behind the scenes
and beyond, where all is light. I say, grip my
hand always, for it is always laid in yours. Get
from me some of the joy you give, — some of the

light and strength. I am overflowing with love, which is force, and you must take from me for my sake. Everywhere there is love, vast treasures of love, that people deny and conceal, but cannot kill, and in the earth and sea also. I am there for you, and love is there!"

All this is the purest sentiment, and yet young Lodge was not sentimental, and especially disliked sentimentality in literature. He would have ruthlessly burned any verse that offered to him the suggestion of sentimentalism. His idyll was intense because it was as old and instinctive as nature itself, and as simple. If he ever approached a sentimental expression, it was in the relation between parent and child, not between lover and mistress. Love was to him a passion, and a very real one, not capable of dilution or disguise. Such passions generally have their own way, and force everything to yield. The marriage took place in Boston, August 18, 1900. True to his instinct of shrinking from close and serious contact with the forms and conventions of a society which was to him neither a close nor a serious relation, he was married without previous notice, and without other than the necessary witnesses, at the Church of the Advent. The officiating clergyman is said to have remarked that he had never seen a more beautiful wedding; but he was the only person present to appreciate its beauty.

They went off to Concord to pass the honeymoon, and thence to Tuckanuck. All the practical difficulties in their way were ignored, and remained ignored through life, without interfering with the young couple's happiness. The world is still kind to those who are young, and handsome, and in love, and who trample on respectability. Naturally, as soon as the winter came, they set off for Paris.

TO HIS MOTHER

PARIS, *January*, 1901.

We have found a most charming little apartment, furnished — with only the indispensable, thank Heaven! The superfluous in a furnished apartment of modest price is horrible — and for only two hundred francs a month. We took it. It is 46 Rue du Bac. The house is an old palace of the days when the Rue du Bac was a fashionable street. It is built on three sides of an enormous court as wide as Massachusetts Avenue without the sidewalks. At the back of the court are large greenhouses of a florist — very pretty. Our apartment is on the court, on a southwest corner, filled with sun and very nice for us. It is at the top of the house. The stair-case is really splendid, — very large, with three great windows on every landing and fine wrought-iron railing, the first flight in stone, the other two in bricks. The apartment itself is the funniest nicest place you ever saw, a sort of Vie de Bohême poetry about it, and sun and air to waste. The walls are very thick, so that the place is full of closets and the windows are all in deep recesses. Some of the floors are stone, others hard wood. We are delighted with it. The Rue du Bac runs up from the Pont Royal, if you remember, and 46 is near the river, and in fact within striking distance of everywhere. Well, we got the apartment, and you may imagine we have been busy, and Mrs. Cameron has been kindness itself, lending us things to cover the walls, etc. We are having a bully time getting installed and altogether I never had such fun in my life.

And there's for the practical side of things. I have n't got round to the absorbing psychological problems surrounding me, nor to the theatres we've seen, nor the work I've done, — a good deal, — nor the thoughts we've thought.

TO HIS FATHER

PARIS, 1901.

We live quite alone and see hardly any one. I am hard at work on one or two things. The law against religious associations has at last passed and all socialists are happy. The next move is to confiscate Rothschild, then the manufacturers, then the other bourgeois, and so on to socialism. There are one or two new things here which would interest you, I think — such as casts of some of the things found at Delphi, the new bridge over the Seine, Pont Alexandre III, which is really very good, and some other things too.

PARIS, 1901.

I have sent the Louis to Bourgouin, and I will at once attend to the books. The socialists here have

started a "librairie socialiste." How it differs from
an ordinary book-shop neither they nor I know;
but as I live more or less among socialists, I find
myself obliged to get my books there and yours will
be sent from there. Curiously enough it is an excellent shop. I was very glad to hear that you
expect to get through without an extra session. I
had been afraid that Cuba and the Philippines
might delay you and produce discord. You know,
however, how difficult it is to know what is hap-
pening *de par le monde* in this most provincial capital. The New York "Herald" had become merely
a vulgar sort of "Town Topics," published every
day, and has, I really think, less news than the
best French papers. In which connection I should
like extremely to know the truth about the row
Sampson has got himself into. I saw that Allen
attacked him in his usual polished way in the
Senate, which, coupled with the fact that I greatly
admire Sampson, warmed my heart for him. But it
seems impossible to find out what it was all about.

Here the whole of France is shaken over the
pending bill confiscating the property of the reli-

gious orders. It is going to pass and the Church is pretty sick. The debate has produced one interesting piece of statistics: that there are three times as many monks in France now as there were in 1789, whereas the population has not quite doubled. My friend, Hubert, says, "C'est curieux, ça démontre que nous retournions à la barbarie." B—— saw some American colonist lady the other day, who told her that Porter was a very bad ambassador. *B——*. Why? — *American colonist lady.* Because he is pro-Boer. — *B——*. But I thought that was popular in France. — *American colonist lady.* Oh, no, all the Americans here are pro-English. — This strikes me as a very characteristic expression of the American colonist point of view.

We see very few people and no society, and less than no American colony, and we are very happy indeed. We are looking forward very much to your advent on the scene. There are some new plays and things which may amuse you. Also they have at last arranged the great series of Rubenses in the Louvre, as decorations, which is what they are

meant to be. I am writing a good deal and studying the rest of the time. Please give my love to
Theodore when he takes the veil. I hope it will be
a fine day for him.

PARIS, 1901.

I am so glad you got through the session so well,
and I hope you are not worn out. I was very much
interested to see that England had refused our
treaty, and I wonder what is coming next. Is the
sentiment strong to abrogate the Clayton-Bulwer
treaty by resolution? I hope so. This refusal really
makes one believe that those whom the Gods wish
to destroy they first make mad.

PARIS, Spring, 1901.

Many, many thanks for your kind letter, and
for all the trouble you have taken about my novel
and my play. I am very glad indeed to have R. S.'s
criticism, and I think that dramatically you and he
are pretty nearly right. Indeed I think the action
in "Villon" is really too subjective for the stage.
It is far more the presentation of an idea than of
an action, and I doubt very much if it can be fitted

for acting. I should be very glad, however, if you would bring it over when you come. I have so much on my hands now that I could not attend to it before then.

The other night I went to hear Jaurès, the Socialist, speak. He is, I think, a very remarkable orator and a very sincere man.

The salon is open here and I have been through it once. There are seven kilometers of canvas, I think, and it's altogether a pretty poor showing, so it seems to me. There are, however, one or two good things, especially in the sculpture, and many clever things.

I hope you will succeed in getting the Bayreuth tickets. We are all very much looking forward to going.

TO HIS MOTHER

PARIS, *Spring*, 1901.

Day before yesterday Hubert took us to St. Germain, where he is "attaché au Musée." It was very interesting and we had a drive in the forest — superb. Hubert is the nicest little man in the world — sympathetic, gentle, bright, and with a preposterous amount of learning. He insists he is going to make me collaborate in some scientific magazine on an Egyptian topic. I hope not. However, I am tolerably strong in Egyptian now. I can read the texts with considerable fluency and the inscriptions on tombs, etc., become very intelligible. It is certainly a useless accomplishment, but excessively interesting. At the same time I have been reading up Chaldea and Syria, Babylonia, etc., so that I have a pretty good idea of the classic Orient. It's a point of departure I have always lacked and needed. Meanwhile, I have written considerably. I enclose a couple of things you may like to see. I am very glad the "Atlantic" and "Century" received me so well. I have just received Papa's letter with the letter from Gilder, and shall answer it at once. Gissing has gone away, I am sorry to say. I should have been glad to see more of him. He is a real man.

CHAPTER VI

"CAIN"

THE European part of the idyll ended with a week at Baireuth and the return home in August, 1901. Thenceforward, the life at Washington in winter, and at Nahant or Tuckanuck in summer, — the life of husband and father, — becomes only the background for literary work, and the work alone remains to tell of the life. The poet's education was finished; what the poet could do with it remains to be shown.

The first result appeared in the volume already mentioned, entitled "Poems (1899–1902)," which appeared in the winter of 1902–03. The next was "Cain," published in November, 1904. The first volume, of one hundred and fifty pages, consisted of the short efforts of the poet's youth. The second volume is a single, sustained effort of drama, and claimed attention less for its poetic than for its dramatic qualities.

Like all the poets of the same school, Lodge con-

ceded nothing to mere decoration or ornament.
The vigorous standards of this severe Academy regarded a popular or conventional flower as a blot.
Every verse must have its stress, or strain, and
every thought its intensity. This preliminary condition is something not to be discussed, but to be
accepted or rejected in advance, like the conditions
of a color-scheme, or an architectural or musical
composition; and, since few readers are trained to
such technical appreciation, at a moment when the
public refuses to make any mental effort that it
can avoid, the poet's audience is very small. In
reality the mental effort of reading is much less
than that of listening to Wagner or Debussy; but
the poet numbers his audience by scores, while the
musician, if he gets any audience at all, numbers
it by thousands. These restraints are a part of the
given situation under which the dramatic poet
works; conditions which he cannot change; they
are in reality far more severe and paralyzing than
the conditions imposed by the old unities. They
must be kept in mind by the reader, unless his
reading is to be waste of time.

So, too, the dramatic idea is a condition given
beforehand, to be accepted or refused as a whole.
The poet does not want an audience that looks for
gems, — that selects a pretty song or verse, and
rejects the whole, — the unity. He has some one
great tragic motive, which he tries to work out in a
way he thinks his own, and he wants to be judged
by his dramatic effect, as an actor is judged by his
power of holding an audience. Properly he would
ask, not whether his drama is liked, but whether it
is dramatic; not whether the reader was pleased,
but whether he was bored.

Lodge's dramatic motive was always the same,
whether in "Cain," or in "Herakles," or in the
minor poems. It was that of Schopenhauer, of
Buddhism, of Oriental thought everywhere, — the
idea of Will, making the universe, but existing
only as subject. The Will is God; it is nature; it is
all that is; but it is knowable only as ourself. Thus
the sole tragic action of humanity is the Ego, —
the Me, — always maddened by the necessity of
self-sacrifice, the superhuman effort of lifting himself and the universe by sacrifice, and, of course, by

destroying the attachments which are most vital,
in order to attain. The idea is a part of the most
primitive stock of religious and philosophical
motives, worked out in many forms, as Prometheus,
as Herakles, as Christ, as Buddha, — to mention
only the most familiar, — but, in our modern conception of life, impossible to realize except as a
form of insanity. All Saviors were anarchists, but
Christian anarchists, tortured by the self-contra-
dictions of their rôle. All were insane, because
their problem was self-contradictory, and because,
in order to raise the universe in oneself to its highest power, its negative powers must be paralyzed
or destroyed. In reality, nothing was destroyed;
only the Will — or what we now call Energy —
was freed and perfected.

This idea, which probably seemed simpler than
shower or sunshine to a Hindoo baby two thousand
years ago, has never taken root in the western mind
except as a form of mysticism, and need not be
labored further. It was what the French call the
donnée of Lodge's drama, — the condition to be
granted from the start; and it had, for a dramatist,

the supreme merit of being the most universal tragic motive in the whole possible range of thought. Again and again, from varied points of view, Lodge treated it in varied moods and tempers; but his two dramas, "Cain" and "Herakles," were elaborately developed expansions of the theme.

The general reader, who reads a Greek drama in the same spirit in which he reads the morning newspaper, can scarcely get beyond the first half-dozen pages of such a theme; and, in fact, the subject was never intended for him. The more serious student, who reads further, can seldom escape a sense of discomfort from the excessive insistence on the motive, — the violence with which it is — over and over again — thrust before his eyes in its crudest form; and, in fact, Lodge has what the French call the faults of his qualities; he is exuberant, and exuberance passes the bounds of *mesure*. Nature herself is apt to exaggerate in the same way. We must take it — or reject it — as we take a thunderstorm or a flood; it may be unnecessary, but is it dramatic?

Every just critic will leave the reader to answer this question for himself. Taste is a matter about which the Gods themselves are at odds. American taste is shocked by every form of paradox except its own. Greek taste was lavish of paradox, especially about the Gods. Saturn ate his children, and Zeus dethroned his father. Questions of taste! while Lodge's paradox, as developed in Cain, was a question rather of logic, — even almost of mathematics. Step by step, like a demonstration in geometry, the primitive man is forced into the attitude of submission to destiny or assertion of self, and Lodge develops each step as a necessary sequence, in the nature of the Greek fate, but a result of conscious Will. The paradox that Cain killed Abel because, from the beginning, man had no choice but to make himself slave of nature or its master, is, after all, nothing like so paradoxical as the philanthropist idea that man has gone on killing himself since the world began, without any reason at all.

This, then, is the paradox of Cain which Lodge undertook to work out, as Byron had worked it out before him, in one of his strongest dramas; and the readers who take it in this sense can hardly fail to find it dramatic. They may not like the drama, but they will probably not toss it aside. They will admit its force. They may even, if particularly sensitive to this oldest of emotional motives, follow the poet himself to the end.

> Captain, my Soul, despair is not for thee!
> Thou shalt behold the seals of darkness lift,
> Weather the wrathful tempest and at last,
> Resolute, onward, headlong, dazed and scarred,
> Reel through the gates of Truth's enormous dawn!

To develop this idea in its dramatic form, Lodge took as his text the words of Genesis, and allowed himself only the four characters, Adam, Eve, Cain and Abel. He gave himself no favors; he introduced no light tones; on his sombre background the figures move in no more light than is strictly necessary to see them move at all; they follow the rules of the mediæval Mystery Play, rather than those of the Greek drama. Yet any sympathetic workman of literary effect will probably admit that they do move, and even that at certain moments their movement is highly dramatic; so much so as to be genuinely emotional.

So also with the characters themselves! If there is a character hard to deal with in the whole range of dramatic effort, Adam is he! No artist has succeeded in making Adam sympathetic, and very few indeed have tried to do so. "The woman tempted me and I did eat" has been his sentence of condemnation as a figure of drama, since drama was acted. Such a figure could not be heroic, and only with difficulty could be saved from being ridiculous on the stage. Even the twelfth-century "Mystery of Adam's Fall" dwelt only on his weakness and abject submission to Eve on one side, and to God on the other. Lodge accepted the traditional figure, and made the best of it.

> Though my life is bruised with sore affliction
> And dire repentance blast my happiness;
> Though in remembrance Paradise forever
> Blooms with fresh light and flowers ineffable,
> Clear pieties and peaceful innocence,
> Against the gloom of this grieved sentience
> Of violence and starvation, yet I bear,

Scornful of tears, the grief and scorn of life!
Faith is the stern, austere acknowledgment
And dumb obedience to the will of God:
Such faith my soul has kept inviolable!
What though he crush me, is not He the Lord!

The drama permitted little development of
Adam's character: he scarcely appears after the
first act, leaving the stage to the two brothers to
work out their inevitable antagonism, and their
contradictory conceptions of duty. Although
Cain's character necessarily had to be developed
to the point of insanity, it was a logical insanity;
while Abel's character remained also true to its
logical conditions of submission to a force or will
not its own. The two brothers represented two
churches, and the strife ended as such strife in history has commonly ended, — in the destruction of
one or the other, the victory of faith or free-will.

The character which Lodge developed with evident sympathy was not masculine but feminine.
Cain might be himself, but Eve was the mother, a
nature far more to his liking. Upon her was thrown
the whole burden and stress of the men's weakness

or insanity. The drama opens upon her, bearing
the alternate reproaches and entreaties of Adam,
and trying to infuse into him a share of her own
courage and endurance; Adam implores her: —

> "Hold me — I need thy tenderness, I need
> Thy calm and pitiful hands to comfort me."

Eve answers: —

> "Be still a little; all will be well, I know."

A total inversion of rôles! and it is carried
through consistently to the end. All the men appeal to Eve, and then refuse to listen to her. In
the vehement dispute at the end of the first act,
Adam at last turns to Eve, and bids her to lecture
her son: —

> And thou, Eve, Woman, most perilously wandered
> In weak delusion, now I charge thee speak —
> Lest thou should fall again in deathless sin, —
> Of God and man, — God's all, man's nothingness!
>
> EVE
> Dear son, we are God's creatures every one —
>
> CAIN
> Mother!
>
> EVE
> I'll speak no more! —

Except perhaps the somewhat undeveloped figure of Abel, all these characters are personally
felt, — to the dramatist they were real and living
figures, — but that of Eve is the most personal of
all. As the drama opens on the wife bearing the
reproaches and supporting the weakness of the
husband, so it ends by the mother assuming the
insanities of the son. After the traditional development of the mediæval drama, Eve is reproduced
in the Virgin. Lodge adhered closely to the mediæval scheme except in transposing the rôles of the
brothers, and intensifying the rôle of the mother.
As, in the mediæval conception, the rôle of the Virgin almost effaced the rôle of Christ, the drama of
Cain ends by almost effacing Cain in the loftier
self-sacrifice of the woman: —

> "Go forth, go forth, lonely and godlike man!
>   My heart will follow tho' my feet must stay.
>   Yet in thy solitude shall there be a woman
>   To care for thee through the incessant days,
>   To lie beside thee in the desolate nights,
>   To love thee as thy soul shall love the truth!
>   In her thy generation shall conceive
>   Passionate daughters, strong and fierce-eyed sons,

> To lift the light and bear the labor of truth
> Whereof the spark is mine, the fire is thine."

Perhaps some readers would find more meaning and higher taste in the drama had Lodge called it "Eve" instead of calling it "Cain"; but here the dramatist was developing his theme in philosophy rather than in poetry, and the two motives almost invariably stand in each other's light. The maternal theme is the more poetic and dramatic, but without the philosophy the poem and the drama have no reason to exist. The reader must take it as it is given, or must throw it aside altogether, and compose a drama of his own, with a totally different *donnée*. In either case, he will search long, and probably in vain, through American literature, for another dramatic effort as vigorous and sustained as that of "Cain," and, if he finds what he seeks, it is somewhat more than likely that he will end by finding it in "Herakles."

CHAPTER VII

THE GREAT ADVENTURE

COMPOSITION, and especially dramatic composition, is an absorbing task. Night passes rapidly in shaping a single phrase, and dawn brings a harsh light to witness putting it in the fire. Lodge worked habitually by night, and destroyed as freely as he composed. Meanwhile life went on, with such pleasures and pains as American life offers; but, in narrative, the pains take the larger place, and the pleasures are to be understood as a background. The most serious loss to Lodge's life was the illness and death of his friend, Trumbull Stickney, whose companionship had been his best support since the early days of Paris and the Latin Quarter. Stickney owned a nature of singular refinement, and his literary work promised to take rank at the head of the work done by his generation of Americans; but he had hardly come home to begin it at Harvard College when he was struck

down by fatal disease. Lodge's letters had much
to say of the tragedy, and of the volume of verses
which he helped to publish afterwards in order to
save what relics remained of Stickney's poetry.

From Boston in August, 1904, he wrote his wife:
"Just after I wrote to you, John called me up on
the telephone and told me that Joe [Stickney] was
very seriously ill at the Victoria. I went down
there at once and saw Lisel, the doctor, and Lucy,
and I write to you now, in the greatest agony of
mind. Joe has got a tumor on the brain. For ten
days he has had almost constant terrific pains in
his head. They brought him to Boston last Thurs-
day. You can imagine how dreadful a shock it
was to get this frightful news when I had hoped to
take Joe to Tuckanuck with us. I am completely
unnerved. . . . The doctor told me I should certainly not be able to see him—no one can. . . .
I feel at present utterly prostrated. Somehow I
have never conceived of Joe's dying."

From Tuckanuck, September 1: "You can
imagine better than I can tell you, with what a
tense and anxious hope I cling to the possibility

that Joe will be saved, and returned to life a well man. I feel almost heart-broken when I think of him, and my mind goes back through all the immense days and ways of life that we have seen together. . . . Doc [Sturgis Bigelow] is, as you may guess, the best and dearest companion in this twilight of grief and anxiety in which I have my present being, and this place is of course more soothing than anywhere else to me. . . ."

From Nahant, November, 1904: "Don't get carried away with the idea that Joe's death has set the term to youth or is really the end of anything. Life — our life, his life, the life of the human soul — is quite continuous, I'm convinced: one thing with another, big and little, sad and gay, real and false, and the whole business just life, which is its own punishment and reward, its own beginning and end. . . ."

From Nahant, November, 1904: "I've finished re-reading the 'Republic,' and it is one of the few books in which my sons shall be thoroughly educated if I can manage it. There are not more than a very few books from which every man can catch

a glimpse of the Great Idea, for there are only a
very few great torch-bearers. But the 'Republic' is one, and much more accessible than any
other, except the 'Leaves of Grass'; for Christ is
deeply hidden in the rubbish of the Church, and
Buddha and Liao Tze are very far removed from
the processes of our minds."

From Boston, January, 1905: "I've had the
most warm and vivid delight in Dok's [Sturgis
Bigelow's] company, which has been constantly
with me since I came here. He has surpassed himself in kindness and clear, warm, wise sympathy
and comprehensiveness. To-night I have passed a
long and superb evening with him, in which we
have together, in a manner of speaking, *fait le tour*
on the parapets of thought. It has renewed and
inspired me, given me, as it were, a new departure
and a new vista. . . . I hate to leave to-morrow,
for he seems so glad to have me, and I, the Gods
know, get everything from being with him. He
does, as you might say, continually see me through,
— through confusion, and through mistakes and
desperations, — in fact, through life. It's im-

mense, what he has done and does for me. In short, after two days of him I feel all straightened out, and you, you best know how badly I needed this beneficent process. Last night we saw Réjane in 'L'Hirondelle,' a play not at all superior, not of any brilliancy of merit or originality of human criticism, but so, after all, interesting by virtue of a certain apparent and immense genuine reality, — so 'written,' with such glitter of words and phrase and epigram, and so acted, above all, that we both passed an evening of immense, contented, uncritical delight."

From Mrs. Wharton's, New York, January, 1905: "I left Boston rather sadly, for my days there had been marvellous. A real readjustment and recoherence of all the immense pressure of great experience which has, as you know, kept me struggling and a little breathless since Joe's death. With Dok I really found my footing, brushed the night from my eyes, and took a long glance forward. . . . Mrs. Wharton was really glad to see me, and I to see her, and we have had a good deal of the swift, lucid, elliptical conversation which is so perfect and so stimulating and so neatly defined in its range. . . . It is a great delight to be with her, as I am a good deal, and to be clear and orderly and correct in one's thought and speech, as far as one goes. It's good for one, and vastly agreeable besides, — indeed, it is to me a kind of gymnastic excitement, very stimulating."

As these letters show, the death of Stickney threw Lodge rather violently back on himself and his personal surroundings, and he stretched out his hands painfully for intellectual allies. A stroke of rare good fortune threw a new friend in his way, to fill the void in his life that Stickney had left. Langdon Mitchell, another poet and dramatist, with much the same ideals and difficulties, but with ten years' more experience, brought him help and counsel of infinite value, as his letters show: —

TO LANGDON MITCHELL

NAHANT (*July*, 1903).

DEAR MITCHELL, — Before receiving your letter and in an ecstasy of good manners, I wrote to your wife to ask her if I might come to you on the 17th. I can't very well come earlier for I am by way of seeing my parents off to Europe, where my Dad is going to assist in despoiling the virtuous Briton, for whom the wrathful tears of the State Department abundantly flow, of what neither is nor ought to be his except on the theory that everything of value should belong to that people who, when pressed, will blushingly confess that they are the chosen of God. My father starts, then, on this engaging mission [1] on the 17th, and after having given him my blessing and those counsels gained only by inexperience, without which no child with any sense of responsibility should take leave of his father, having in fact done all my duty, I shall at once turn myself to pleasure and embark with a mind wholly vague as to direction, you-ward. It's mighty good of you, dear Mitchell, and of your wife too to want me for a few days, and I can't tell you with how great pleasure I look forward to seeing you. We 'll have some great days.

[1] The Alaskan Boundary Tribunal, which met in London in the summer of 1903 and of which his father was a member.

1925 F St., *October, 1903.*

DEAR MITCHELL, — Good! You understand
Beaudelaire as I do; indeed you say things about
him which make me realize as never before my own
comprehension of him. I am doubtful about
French poetry being, like Latin, "City poetry."
Think of Ronsard and his crowd, or Victor Hugo
or Leconte de Lisle — but Beaudelaire, like Villon,
like Verlaine, is certainly a city poet. And why not?
The civilization of an old society is, I am certain,
the fair material of poems. The best is that Beaudelaire has given you pleasure, and I feel that you
have appreciated as I do that he is, in his best moments, really a great poet, one of the torch-bearers.
"Allons! after the great companions and to belong
to them!" Ah! let us go and be of them if we can,
dear Mitchell. At least we can follow on the "great
road of the Universe." Which reminds me that I
have been reading your verses again and again and
I shall have, for what they're worth, some remarks
to make when we next meet.

1925 F St., *Spring*, 1904.

DEAR MITCHELL, — I largely agree with what
you say of Viele's book, though to my mind you
rate it a little too high. His delight in words seems
to me far his strongest trick. He says not very
much. Of course keep Cain till April 1st or as long
as you wish. As you may imagine, all that you say
about it in your letter is deeply interesting to me.
As I've said to you, you are the only person from
whom I expect genuine criticism and get it. As
regards the stage directions I'll say this: Although
the thing has no quality of a real play, nevertheless
the action — that is, the main points of the action
— are essential to the expression of the idea, and
therefore it is necessary that there should be some
environment indicated, and that the characters
should perform certain motions (as few as possible,
of course). The question, then, is merely this:
whether the poem is more or less interrupted
and the reader subjected to more or less of a jar,
by having environment and action indicated as
briefly and technically as possible, in brackets, or
by having them introduced as verse into the body

of the poem. It seemed to me, despite the obvious absurdities, the former was the method most frank and honest, and least likely to mar the poetic and intellectual integrity of the whole. Of course the mere technicalities could be eliminated if they seriously jarred. Thank you — I wish I could — for all that you say, which I find very just and of the utmost assistance to me in clarifying and enlightening my own criticism; and thank you, above all, for your interest, which is valuable to me beyond words.

I'm mighty sorry but not very greatly surprised to hear your news of the condition of the stage. It's depressing beyond measure to know that the American theatre is reserved exclusively, either for importations, or the worthless manufactures of almost illiterate Americans who regard, plays merely as merchandise, and who would manufacture boots with equal enjoyment and success. Indeed it's most depressing; and what is to be done? Your assertion that the American public will take good plays as well as bad is I believe quite correct, but unfortunately it does n't help as long as they'll take bad plays as well as good. The stage situation is to me merely another sign of the intellectual, moral and spiritual childishness of the American. Indeed was there ever such an anomaly as the American man? In practical affairs his cynicism, energy and capacity are simply stupefying, and in every other respect he is a sentimental idiot possessing neither the interest, the capacity, nor the desire for even the most elementary processes of independent thought. Consider for one moment his position as a domestic animal as it was fifty years ago and as it is to-day. Then he was the unquestioned head of his family, the master of his house, the father of as many children as he wanted to have. His wife's business was to bear his children and manage his household to suit him, and she never questioned it. To-day he is absolutely dethroned. A woman rules in his stead. His wife finds him so sexually inapt that she refuses to bear him children and so drivelling in every way except as a money-getter that she compels him to expend his energies solely in that direction while she leads a discontented, sterile, stunted life, not because

she genuinely prefers it but because she cannot
find a first-rate *man* to make her desire to be the
mother of his children and to live seriously and
happily. I speak of course only of the well-to-do
classes, which as a matter of fact comprise most
real Americans, and of which the average number
of children per family is under two. We are, dear
Mitchell, a dying race, as every race must be of
which the men are, as men and not accumulators,
third-rate. American women don't fall in love with
the American men (I mean, really) and they're
quite right; only a woman won't have children by
a man she's not really in love with, and when you
think of the travail and the peril of death can you
blame her? It's an odd situation; we are a dying
race and really we've never lived.

Forgive this long dissertation. I got started and
could not stop.

1925 F St., *April*, 1904.

DEAR MITCHELL, — I'm nearly in a position
now to answer the question which we discussed —
perhaps you remember — last summer at Tuckanuck: namely whether or not Jesus Christ ap-

peared as the logical outcome of the Jewish religious tradition. You remember I contended he was wholly sporadic and attached to nothing. I begin now to see I was in a measure quite wrong, and perhaps to a small extent right. I am very anxious to talk it over with you when you return here, and also to discuss with you the whole state of thought and feeling in Judæa at the time of Christ's appearance. All this, you will guess, is the result of work I've been doing in preparation for writing the Christ-play of which I spoke to you and which, to my immense delight, you seem to approve — at least the idea — in your last letter. I've already gone far enough to realize that no subject could be more fascinating or more interesting. Jesus Christ and his teachings, which are neglected and unknown, form a background against which the dark threads of the lives and passions and thoughts of worldly men should stand out like the black bars on the solar spectrum. I have re-read Renan's "Vie de Jésus" and it's interesting in many ways and a "beau livre"; but, dear Mitchell, can you imagine a man spending ten years on the study of Jesus Christ and at last summing up his appreciation of the man in this phrase: "C'est un charmeur!" It's staggering.

1925 F St. (*Spring of* 1904).

DEAR MITCHELL, — I imagine what you say of solitude is very true. "Tout se paie" — in one form or another. Certainly you have kept singularly balanced, singularly vital and sane — in the true sense. What I shall be in ten years there's no guessing. One stakes one's life on the chance of ransoming "one lost moment with a rhyme" and the wheel turns —

Of course keep "Cain" as long as you want. I really feel ashamed to bother you with it when you are so busy, but it's vastly important to me to know precisely what you think; whether, in your deliberate opinion, it's the real thing in any degree whatever, and not merely and utterly — literature! But don't, I beg you, look at it until it's convenient. I shan't write another long thing in verse for some time. Since publishing "Cain" I've had a time of horrible reaction and "abattement"

— the sort of thing we all go through occasionally. This has become a drearily egotistical and dull letter. . . .

My days in New York were glorious, the only good days I've had since finishing that poem. I need hardly say how deeply I hope you will dispose of your plays to your satisfaction — for your sake and for the sake of the stage.

1925 F St., WASHINGTON
(Spring, 1904).

I think, dear Mitchell, that we really about agree as to the Sonnet. The first rate ones are terribly few and in diverse forms. Witness Beaudelaire.

.   .   .   .

My dear man, I've got hold of such a splendid thing to write — immense. I'm shutting down on Society, in which we've been wandering this winter to the detriment of all I value in life, and I'm getting to work — God be praised. I wish I could have a talk with you about this and so many other things. One gets glimpses, such glimpses, of incredible, tremendous things. I wish you were by so we might share them. I feel always tempted to run over for a day to see you, but I'm afraid it's quite impossible now. Still if the desire pushes me too hard I'll turn up some afternoon. Spring-Rice has been here for a week and I had one splendid talk with him and wished more than ever you were here. There's a man who does, really, keep up wonderfully and by a very peculiar faculty he has of remaining, au fond, quite detached from his own circumstances and experience. He left to-night, alas! He goes back to Russia, about which he had absorbing things to say. Now that he's gone, once more the "void weighs on us," — the dreadful, blank, mild nothingness of this nice agreeable, easy, spacious vacuity (comp. James). And here I am again alone beyond belief, but, fortunately, with a very interesting thing to do, so I'm very well off.

NAHANT, MASS., *October*, 1904.

DEAR MITCHELL, — I was extremely glad to get your note and I would have answered it before had not events compelled me. On the eleventh my friend Stickney died — quite suddenly at the last.

On the fourteenth we buried him. He was thirty
years old — by far the most promising man I have
known, his best work still and surely to come.
Under the terrible test of a mortal disease his
mind and character rose to higher levels than
they had ever touched before. He died, really, at
the height of his powers. The future held nothing
for him but suffering, mental and physical. He is
very well out of it. Dear Mitchell, what a life
it is! — what a life! I am having an undoubtedly
hard time. So, it must be said, are other people.

I wish I could get to New York now and see you.
I feel more deeply than ever how invaluable your
friendship is to me and how incalculably better
than anything else in life, such friendship as I
think you and I share together is in the last analysis. I would come if I had the energy, but I am
pretty well done up morally and physically. I
shall be in New York, though, from November 9th
for some days. Could n't you be there then too?
It would be to me so true a happiness to see you
again.

Naturally, too, in the social and literary sequence, young Lodge fell under the charm of Henry James: —

WASHINGTON, *May*, 1905.

To this even existence of mine there has been one delightful interruption, namely the lecture and subsequent visions of Henry James. The lecture was profoundly, and to one who writes himself, wonderfully interesting; so many splendid things which had been long at home in my own consciousness and which I first heard then, perfectly and irresistibly expressed. The amiable Miss T——had asked us to tea for the next day; where I went and found, besides James, old Mrs. ——, a most original and charming and distinguished person, conveying, through all her rather stiff but flattering courtesy, the vivid impression that she might be, on occasion, equally original and the reverse of charming. There were besides some unremarkable people who all left, leaving me the chance to talk with James, which I did with the greatest delight then and also the next morning when, at his invitation, I went with him to the Capitol and the Library for two most interesting hours. This, I believe, can be said of James, though it is not the most obvious remark to make of him, and is, at the same time, the rarest and most important compliment that can be paid to any creative artist — namely, that he is, in matters of art, incorruptibly honest, and in consequence hugely expensive. He is, I mean, as an artist, built through and through of the same material — which you like or not according to your fancy. His very style — again whether you like it or not — bears by its mere tortuous originality, if by no other sign, infallible witness that he has, at immense expenditure, done all the work — artistically and intellectually — and that all the work is his own. In ideas and art he lives in a palace built of his own time and thought, while the usual, you might say the ubiquitous, average person and literary prostitute lives contentedly in one of an interminable row of hovels, built, so to speak, on an endless contract from bare material stolen from Time's intellectual scrapheap. What it all amounts to is that, whether you

like James or not, whether you think he is all on
the wrong track or not, you are bound to respect
him, for if you do not, whom, in this age of universal machine-made cheapness, whom more than
James with his immense talent and industry *and*
his small sales, are you going to respect?

This is a long garrulous, egotistical (to a degree),
and perhaps you will say, rather incoherent letter.
So I will spare you any further palpitating details
of my obscure life.

WASHINGTON, *June,* 1905.

Indeed, I wish I might have been with you, but
on the other hand I have done an immense deal by
being quietly and in much long solitude just now
at this time. I have lived high most of my working
hours, and in consequence my volume of sonnets
— "The Great Adventure," I call it, which is, I
think, a good title — lies before me all but finished
— seventy-five sonnets or more, with which I am
pretty well pleased. I feel lonely, as I always do
when I am hard at work, but I also feel much ex-
hilaration. These are my great years. Well, I am
sure I must have said all this before to you. **My**

interest in myself is so poignant that I elude it with difficulty.

Joe's volume represents for me a good deal of work and an experience of grief that neither gives nor receives consolation, which has left its indelible mark upon me — which is good. For I believe there are but two ways with real grief: get rid of it if you can; but if you can't, then take all you can get of it, live in it, work in it, experience it as far as you are capable of experiencing anything. Let it nourish you! as it will, as anything will that is real, and in direct proportion to its reality and significance. I'll tell you that I sent my volume of sonnets to Houghton & Mifflin, who wrote me that they held my work in high consideration; which, I suppose, indicates that some people they have seen think well of "Cain." Also, perhaps you have seen "Moriturus" (by me) in the July "Scribner."

"The Great Adventure" was published in October, — a small volume of ninety pages, of which nearly one third were devoted to the memory of Stickney: —

He said: "We are the Great Adventurers;
This is the Great Adventure : thus to be
Alive, and, on the universal sea
Of being, lone yet dauntless mariners.

.   .   .   .

This is the Great Adventure!" All of us
Who saw his dead, deep-visioned eyes, could see,
After the Great Adventure, immanent,
Splendid and strange, the Great Discovery.

Love and Death were the two themes of these sonnets, almost as personal as the "Song of the Wave." Underneath the phrases and motives of each, lay almost always the sense of striving against the elements, like Odysseus, or against the mysteries, like Plato: —

"At least," he said, "we spent with Socrates
Some memorable days, and in our youth
Were curious and respectful of the Truth,
Thrilled with perfections and discoveries,
And with the everlasting mysteries
We were irreverent and unsatisfied, —
And so we are!" he said . . .

The irreverence mattered little, since it was mostly the mere effervescence of youth and health; but the dissatisfaction went deep, and made a

serious strain on his energy, — a strain which
Stickney's death first made vital. The verses began to suggest discouragement: —

> In Time's cathedral, Memory, like a ghost,
> Crouched in the narrow twilight of the nave,
> Fumbles with thin pathetic hands to save
> Relics of all things lived and loved and lost.
> Life fares and feasts, and Memory counts the cost
> With unrelenting lips that dare confess
> Life's secret failures, sins and loneliness,
> And life's exalted hopes, defiled and crossed.

"The Great Adventure" probably marked the
instant when life did, in fact, hover between the
two motives, — the beginning and the end, —
Love and Death. Both were, for the moment, in
full view, equally near, and equally intense, with
the same background of the unknown: —

> In the shadow of the Mystery
> We watched for light with sleepless vigilance,
> Yet still, how far soever we climbed above
>   The nether levels, always, like a knife,
>   We felt the chill of fear's blind bitter breath;
> For still a secret crazed the heart of Love,
>   An endless question blurred the eyes of Life,
>   A baffling silence sealed the lips of Death.

Meanwhile life went on with what most people would, at least in retrospect, regard as altogether exceptional happiness. The small circle of sympathetic companions was immensely strengthened by the addition of Edith Wharton, whose unerring taste and finished workmanship served as a corrective to his youthful passion for license. Her fine appreciation felt this quality as the most insistent mark of his nature: —

"Abundance, — that is the word which comes to me whenever I try to describe him. During the twelve years of our friendship, — and from the day that it began, — I had, whenever we were together, the sense of his being a creature as profusely as he was finely endowed. There was an exceptional delicacy in his abundance, and an extraordinary volume in his delicacy."

Life is not wholly thrown away on ideals, if only a single artist's touch catches like this the life and movement of a portrait. Such a picture needs no proof; it is itself convincing.

"The man must have had a sort of aura about him. Perhaps he was one of those who walk on the

outer rim of the world, aware of the jumping-off
place; which seems the only way to walk, — but
few take it. Odd that your article should have
appealed so much to me, when I know so little of
the subject!"

The more competent the reader, — and this
reader, though unnamed, was among the most
competent, — the more complete is the conviction;
and the same simple quality of the truest art runs
through the whole of Mrs. Wharton's painting,
to which the critic was alluding. Every touch of
her hand takes the place of proof.

"All this," she continues, "on the day when he
was first brought to see me, — a spring afternoon
of the year 1898, in Washington, — was lit up by
a beautiful boyish freshness, which, as the years
passed, somehow contrived to ripen without fading. In the first five minutes of our talk, he *gave*
himself with the characteristic wholeness that
made him so rare a friend; showing me all the sides
of his varied nature; the grave sense of beauty, the
flashing contempt of meanness, and that large
spring of kindly laughter that comes to many only

as a result of the long tolerance of life. It was one of his gifts thus to brush aside the preliminaries of acquaintance, and enter at once, with a kind of royal ease, on the rights and privileges of friendship; as though — one might think — with a foreboding of the short time given him to enjoy them.

"Aside from this, however, there was nothing of the pathetically predestined in the young Cabot Lodge. Then — and to the end — he lived every moment to the full, and the first impression he made was of a joyous physical life. His sweet smile, his easy strength, his deep eyes full of laughter and visions, — these struck one even before his look of intellectual power. I have seldom seen anyone in whom the natural man was so wholesomely blent with the reflecting intelligence; and it was not the least of his charms that he sent such stout roots into the earth, and had such a hearty love for all he drew from it. Nothing was common or unclean to him but the vulgar, the base, and the insincere, and his youthful impatience at the littleness of human nature was tempered by an unusually mature sense of its humors."

While young Lodge, or any other young artist,
might find it the most natural thing in the world
to give himself without thought or hesitation to
another artist, like Mrs. Wharton, it by no means
followed that he could give himself to men or women who had not her gifts, or standards, or sympathies. He could no more do this than he could
write doggerel. However much he tried, and the
more he tried, to lessen the gap between himself —
his group of personal friends — and the public, the
gap grew steadily wider; the circle of sympathies
enlarged itself not at all, or with desperate slow-
ness; and this consciousness of losing ground, —
of failure to find a larger horizon of friendship beyond his intimacy; — the growing fear that, beyond this narrow range, no friends existed in the
immense void of society, — or could exist, in the
form of society which he lived in, — the suffocat-
ing sense of talking and singing in a vacuum that
allowed no echo to return, grew more and more
oppressive with each effort to overcome it. The
experience is common among artists, and has often
led to violent outbursts of egotism, of self-assertion,

of vanity; but the New England temper distrusts itself as well as the world it lives in, and rarely yields to eccentricities of conduct. Emerson himself, protesting against every usual tendency of society, respected in practice all its standards.

"One is accustomed," continued Mrs. Wharton, "in enjoying the comradeship of young minds, to allow in them for a measure of passing egotism, often the more marked in proportion to their sensitiveness to impressions; but it was Cabot Lodge's special grace to possess the sensitiveness without the egotism. Always as free from pedantry as from conceit, he understood from the first the give and take of good talk, and was not only quick to see the other side of an argument, but ready to reinforce it by his sympathetic interpretation. And because of this responsiveness of mind, and of the liberating, vivifying nature from which it sprang, he must always, to his friends, remain first of all, and most incomparably, a Friend."

This quality was strongly felt by others. One who knew him intimately when he was Secretary of the British Embassy in Washington and later when they were together in Berlin, Sir Cecil Spring-Rice, now minister of Great Britain in Stockholm, wrote of him after his death: —

"The first time I saw him was at Nahant when the children were all there together; and since then I have always seemed to know him closely and intimately. We bathed together there, and I remember so well the immense joy he had in jumping into the water, and then lying out in the sun till he was all browned — as strong and healthy a human creature as I have ever seen, and exulting in his life. Then we rode together at Washington, and I can see him now galloping along in the woody country near Rock Creek. It did n't strike me then that he was anything but a strong healthy boy, absolutely straight, sincere, and natural.

"It was n't till I saw a good deal of him in Berlin that I realized what a rare and extraordinary mind he had. He was then studying hard at philosophy. In an extraordinarily quick time he learnt German and seemed to take naturally to the most difficult books — just as he had done to the sea, without any conscious effort. We had many talks then, and his

talk was most inspiring. He constantly lived face
to face with immense problems, which he thought
out thoroughly and earnestly, — things men often
read and study in order to pass examinations or
achieve distinction; but I am quite sure with him
there was no object except just the attainment and
the presence of truth. He had a most living mind,
and a character absolutely independent; resolved
on finding out things by himself, and living by his
own lights and thinking out his own problems.
Nothing would have stopped him or interfered
with him. In all my experience of people about the
world, I never knew any one so 'detached,' deaf to
the usual voices of the world; and so determined
to live in the light of Truth, taking nothing for
granted till he had proved it by his own original
thought. He had greatly developed when I last saw
him in Washington, during the few days I spent
there. I had two long talks with him in his house.
I think he was the sort of stuff that in the middle
ages would have made a great saint or a great
heresiarch — I dare say we have no use for such
people now; I wonder if he found he was born out

of his time, and that ours was not a world for him.
I am not thinking of what he wrote or what he said,
but of the atmosphere in which he lived, and the
surroundings of his own soul — what his thoughts
lived and moved in.

"In that detachment and independence and
courage I have never known any one like him. Yet
it was hardly courage: for he did n't give the enemy a thought.

"I wonder if one often meets a man in these
times who is literally capable of standing alone, to
whom the noises and sights of the world, which
to most people are everything, are nothing, absolutely nothing — the state of mind of some one
who is madly in love, but with him it seemed normal and natural, an everyday habit of being.

"It was only last week I had a long think as I
was walking about through these lonely woods
here, and I was wondering whether I should see
you all soon again, and I was saying to myself: At
any rate Bay will have grown — he won't disap-
point me: he is the sort of man who is bound to get
bigger every day — and he is younger and stronger

than I and he will last. —And about how many
men of his age could one say *that* with certainty,
that time would surely improve and perfect him,
and that with every new meeting one could gain
something new?

"And that is how I thought of him naturally."

Like most of the clever young men of his time,—
Oscar Wilde, Bernard Shaw, Gilbert Chesterton,
—he loved a good paradox, and liked to chase it
into its burrow. "When you are accustomed to
anything, you are estranged from it"; and his supreme gift for liking was never to get accustomed
to things or people. By way of a historical paradox
he maintained that the Church was devised as a
protection against the direct rays of Christ's spirit,
which, undimmed, would compel to action and
change of character. By way of a poetical paradox he loved Walt Whitman to fanaticism, and
quoted, as his favorite description of the world,
Walt's "little plentiful mannikins skipping about
in collars and tailcoats." Yet he sometimes de-
clared that his favorite line in poetry was Swinburne's: —

Out of the golden remote wild west where the sea without shore
  is,
Full of the sunset, and sad, if at all, with the fulness of joy.

Perhaps, too, if he had chosen a verse of poetry
to suggest his own nature, after the description of
Mrs. Wharton he might have found it in another
line of Swinburne's: —

   Some dim derision of mysterious laughter.

However remote he thought himself from his
world, he was, in fact, very much of his literary
time, — and would not have been recognized at all
by any other. Like most of his young contempo-
raries in literature, he loved his paradoxes chiefly
because they served as arrows for him to practise
his art on the social conventions which served for
a target; and the essence of his natural simple-
mindedness showed itself in his love for this boy's-
play of fresh life which he tired of only too soon, as
he will himself tell in his "Noctambulist." He
knew, at bottom, that the world he complained of
had as little faith in its conventions as he had; but,
apart from the fun and easy practice of paradox,

Lodge's most marked trait of mind lay in his instinctive love of logic, which he was probably not even aware of, although often — as is seen everywhere in the "Cain" and "Herakles" — the reasoning is as close and continuous as it might be in Plato or Schopenhauer.

This contrast of purposes disconcerted most readers. The usual reader finds the effort of following a single train of thought too severe for him; but even professional critics rebel against a paradox almost in the degree that it is logical, and find the Greek severity of Prometheus, in its motive, a worse fault than what they call the "excess of loveliness," which, in Shelley, "militates against the awful character of the drama." In modern society, the Greek drama is a paradox; which has not prevented most of the greatest nineteenth-century poets from putting their greatest poetry into that form; and Lodge loved it because of its rigorous logic even more than for its unequalled situations. Lodge could be exuberant enough when he pleased, but what he exacted from his readers was chiefly mind.

With this preamble, such readers as care for intellectual poetry can now take up his work of the years 1906 and 1907, published under the titles, "The Soul's Inheritance" and "Herakles." "The Soul's Inheritance" appeared only after his death, but in the natural order of criticism it comes first. Although the vigor of his verse was greater, there were already signs that his physical strength was less, and that he was conscious of it. His health had begun to cause uneasiness; his heart warned him against strains; but he scorned warnings, and insisted that his health was never better. Submission to an obnoxious fact came hard to him, at all times; but the insidious weakness of literary workmen lies chiefly in their inability to realize that quiet work like theirs, which calls for no physical effort, may be a stimulant more exhausting than alcohol, and as morbid as morphine. The fascination of the silent midnight, the veiled lamp, the smouldering fire, the white paper asking to be covered with elusive words; the thoughts grouping themselves into architectural forms, and slowly rising into dreamy structures, constantly changing, shifting, beautifying their outlines, — this is the subtlest of solitary temptations, and the loftiest of the intoxications of genius.

CHAPTER VIII

"HERAKLES"

"THE SOUL'S INHERITANCE" was a poem delivered before the Phi Beta Kappa Society at Cambridge in 1906, and in delivering it, Lodge discovered in himself a new power that would probably have led him in time into a new field, where he could put himself into closer relations with the world. His delivery was good, his voice admirable, and his power over his audience was evident. He was probably an orator by right of inheritance, though he had never cared to assert the claim, preferring to rest his distinction on his poetry.

In this poem he reiterated his life-long theme that the Soul, or Will, is the supreme energy of life: —

> That here and now, no less for each of us,
> That inward voice, cogent as revelation,
> That trance of truth's sublime discovery,
> Which in the soul of Socrates wrought out
> Gold from the gross ore of humanity,

> Still speak, still hold, still work their alchemy;
> That here and now and in the soul's advance,
> And by the soul's perfection, we may feel
> The thought of Buddha in our mortal brain,
> The human heart of Jesus in our breast,
> And in our will the strength of Hercules!

Again, as always in his poetry, he recurred to the sense of struggle, of —

> The multitudinous menace of the night,

and the soul's need to stand out, —

> Importunate and undissuadable,

over the utmost verge of venture: —

> There in our hearts the burning lamp of love,
> There in our sense the rhythm and amplitude,
> And startled splendor of the seas of song.

This last verse, — the " startled splendor of the seas of song," — was one of the kind in which he delighted, and which he had a rare power of framing, but the thought was ever the same: the Soul of Man was the Soul of God; and it was repeated in various forms in the three sonnets attached to the blank verse: —

Strangely, inviolably aloof, alone,
Once shall it hardly come to pass that we,
As with his Cross, as up his Calvary,
Burdened and blind, ascend and share his throne.

Again it was repeated in the poem called "Pilgrims," delivered at the annual dinner of the New England Society, in New York, December, 1906. The theme, on such an occasion and before such an audience, in the fumes of dinner and tobacco, was adventurous, but Lodge adhered to it bravely, and insisted all the more on its value, —

Lest we grow tired and tame and temperate.

He boldly asserted: "We *are* the Pilgrims," and proved it by attaching to the blank verse three sonnets, as beautiful as he ever wrote: —

They are gone. . . . They have all left us, one by one:
    Swiftly, with undissuadable strong tread,
    Cuirassed in song, with wisdom helmeted,
    They are gone before us, into the dark, alone. . . .
Upward their wings rushed radiant to the sun;
    Seaward the ships of their emprise are sped;
    Onward their starlight of desire is shed;
    Their trumpet-call is forward; — they are gone!
Let us take thought and go! — we know not why
    Nor whence nor where, — let us take wings and fly!

> Let us take ship and sail, take heart and dare!
> Let us deserve at last, as they have done,
>   To say of all men living and dead who share
>   The soul's supreme adventure, — *We* are gone!

These verses appeared in print only after his death, as though he had intended them for his epitaph; and perhaps he did, for he continued in the same tone: —

> Let us go hence! — however dark the way,
>   Haste! — lest we lose the clear, ambitious sense
>   Of what is ours to gain and to gainsay.
> Let us go hence, lest dreadfully we die!

Two poems cast in the same form followed: "Life in Love," and "Love in Life"; which return to the intensely personal theme. Readers who feel the theme will probably feel the poetry as the highest he ever reached in feeling. Again the three sonnets follow, with their studied beauties of expression:

> Her voice is pure and grave as song;
>   Her lips are flushed as sunset skies;
>   The power, the myth, the mysteries
>   Of life and death in silence throng
> The secret of her silences;
>   Her face is sumptuous and strong,
>   And twilights far within prolong
>   The spacious glory of her eyes.

On these themes of Love and Life Lodge had
dwelt without interruption from the start; and
now, suddenly, without apparent steps of transi-
tion, he passed to a new motive, — Doubt! "The
Noctambulist" suggests some change, physical or
moral; some new influence or ripened growth, or
fading youth. Perhaps he would himself have
traced the influence and the change, to the death
of Stickney. Mrs. Wharton says that "in its har-
mony of thought and form, it remains perhaps the
completest product" of his art; and it is certainly
the saddest. The note is struck in the first line: —

That night of tempest and tremendous gloom,

when, —

Across the table, for — it seemed to us —
An age of silence, in the dim-lit room,
Tenantless of all humans save ourselves
Yet seeming haunted, as old taverns are,
With the spent mirth of unremembered men,
He mused at us. . . . And then, "I know! . . . " he said,
"I know! O Youth! . . . I too have seen the world
At sunrise, candid as the candid dew;
        . . . You look abroad,
And see the new adventure wait for you,

Splendid with wars and victories; for you
Trust the masked face of Destiny. But I!
I've turned the Cosmos inside out!" he said;
And on his lips the shadow of a smile
Looked hardly human. . . .

Some two hundred lines of unbroken disillusionment follow, which should not be torn to pieces to make easy quotations; but the passages that here and there suggest autobiography may serve as excuse for cutting up such a poem into fragments which now and then resemble the letters in their spontaneous outbursts.

Yes! and I feel anew the splendid zest
Of youth's brave service in truth's ancient cause,
When, with the self-same thunders that you use,
Edged with a wit — at no time Greek! — I too
Most pleasurably assailed and tumbled down,
With a fine sense of conquest and release,
The poor, one, old, enfeebled, cheerless God
Left to us of our much be-Deitied
And more be-Devilled past . . .
And all's well done I doubt not; though the times
Of life may well seem all too brief to waste!
But this comes later, when we learn, — as learn
We must, if we go forward still from strength
To strength incessantly, — to wage no more

With phantoms of the past fortunate wars;
To die no longer on the barricades
For the true faith; to spend no more the rich
And insufficient days and powers of life
Striving to shape the world and force the facts,
Tame the strong heart, and stultify the soul,
To fit some creed, some purpose, some design
Ingeniously contrived to spare the weak,
Protect the timid and delude the fools. —
                    The time must come
When we can deal in partialities
No more, if truth shall prosper; for we stand
Awfully face to face with just the whole
Secret, — our unrestricted Universe,
Spirit and sense! . . . And then, abruptly then
Swift as a passion, brutal as a blow,
The dark shuts down!

Whether he felt the dark already shutting down,
brutal as a blow, or only divined it from the fate of
Stickney, one need not know. The verses prove
that he felt it personally, for he repeated it again
and again: —

In the strict silence, while he spoke no more,
We heard the tumult of our hearts, and feared
Almost as men fear death, and know not why,
We feared, . . . until at last, while at the closed
Windows the wind cried like a frenzied soul,

He said: — "I too have tried, of mortal life,
The daily brief excursions; . . .
                              and I have felt the one
Utterly loosed and loving woman's heart,
There where the twilight failed and night came on,
Thrill to life's inmost secret on my breast;
And I have known the whole of life and been
The whole of man! The Night is best!"

The letters will show that the "Noctambulist" was meant as "a really new and large and valid departure," which, if followed in its natural direction, should have led to dramatic lyrics and problems more or less in the feeling of "Men and Women"; but, immediately, the "Noctambulist" abuts on "Herakles," which properly closes the cycle. In the "Herakles," the poet exhausted, once for all, the whole range of thought and expression with which his life had begun; it was an immense effort; and in approaching the analysis of this drama, which, in bulk, is nearly equal to all the rest of the poet's writings together, and in sustained stress stands beyond comparison with them, the critic or biographer is embarrassed, like the poet himself, by the very magnitude of the scheme.

Although no reader can be now safely supposed
to know anything of the Greek drama, he must be
assumed to have an acquaintance with Æschylus
and Euripides at least. Something must be taken
for granted, even though it be only the bare agree-
ment that Shelley's "Prometheus Unbound" does
not interfere with "Empedocles on Etna" and
that neither of these Greek revivals jostles against
"Atalanta in Calydon." Here are five or six of the
greatest masterpieces of literature with which a
reader must be supposed to be acquainted; and
perhaps he would do well to keep in mind that, in
bulk, Browning's "The Ring and the Book" is
large enough to contain them all, and the "Herakles" too; while the methods and merits of all are
as distinct and personal as the poets.

The reader, too, who takes up the "Herakles"
for the first time, must be supposed to know that
the plot of the drama is not of the poet's making:
it is 'given, — imposed; and the dramatist has
taken care to quote at the outset the words of the
historian, Diodorus, whose story he meant to follow. Herakles and Creon and Megara are familiar

characters in history as well as on the stage, and
as real as historians can make them. Herakles
did marry Megara, the daughter of Creon, King
of Thebes; he did refuse to obey the orders of
Eurystheus, King of Argos; he was actually — according to the historian — seized with frenzy, and
pierced his children with arrows; he submitted to
the will of God, performed his miracles, freed
Prometheus, and became immortal. All this is
fact, which the Greeks accepted, as they afterwards accepted the facts of the Christ's life and
death, his miracles and immortality; and for the
same reasons: for both were Saviors, Pathfinders,
and Sacrifices.

Lodge took up this dramatic motive, — the
greatest in human experience, — as it was given
him; and so the reader must take it, — or leave it,
— since he has nothing to do with the argument of
the play once he has accepted it. His interest is in
the dramatic development of the action, and the
philosophic development of the thought. As for
the thought, something has already been said; but
the reader must be assumed to know that it is the

oldest thought that seems to have been known
to the human mind, and, in the Christian religion,
is the substantial fact which every Catholic sees
realized before his eyes whenever he goes to mass.
The God who sacrifices himself is one with the vic-
tim. The reader who does not already know this
general law of religion which confounds all the different elements that enter into ordinary sacrifice,
can know neither poetry nor religion. Christ carries the whole of humanity in his person. The
identification of subject and object, of thought
and matter, of will and universe, is a part of the
alphabet of philosophy. The conception of a God
sacrificing himself for a world of which he is himself a part, may be a mystery, — a confusion of
ideas, — a contradiction of terms, — but it has
been the most familiar and the highest expression
of the highest — and perhaps also of the lowest
— civilizations.

The reader's whole concern lies therefore not in
the poem's motive but in its action, — the stages
of its movement, — the skill and power with which
the theme is developed, — the copiousness of the

poet's resources,—the art and scope of his presentation. The critic can do no more than sketch an outline of the difficulties; he cannot attempt to discuss the solutions. Scholars seem inclined to think that Euripides himself failed in his treatment of this theme; that Æschylus scarcely rose quite to its level; and that Shelley used it chiefly as a field on which to embroider beauties wholly his own. Where three of the greatest poets that ever lived have found their highest powers taxed to the utmost, a critic can afford to keep silence.

The play opens at Thebes in the empty agora, at sunset, by a dialogue between the eternal poet and the eternal woman, who serve here in the place of the Greek chorus, each seeking, after the way of poet or woman, for something, — the light, — and so introducing the action, which begins abruptly by a feast in the palace of Creon, the king, who has called his people together to witness his abdication in favor of his son-in-law, Herakles.

Creon is a new creation in Lodge's poetry, — a deliberate effort at character-drawing till now unattempted. Creon is the man-of-the-world, the

administrator, the humorist and sage, who has
accepted all the phases of life, and has reached the
end, which he also accepts, whether as a fact or
a phantasm, — whatever the world will, — but
which has no more value to him than as being the
end, neither comprehended nor comprehensible,
but human. Perhaps it is only a coincidence that
Æschylus vaguely suggested such a critic in
Okeanos, who appears early in the "Prometheus."
Creon speaks, "in an even, clear, quiet voice": —

I am your King; and I am old, — and wise.

. . . .

And I can now afford your censure! Yes,
I can afford at last expensive things
Which cost a man the kingdoms of the world,
And all their glory! I have lived my life;
— You cannot bribe me now by any threat
Of ruin to my life's high edifice,
Or any dazzled prospect of ambition. . . .
I think despite these sceptical strange words,
You will respect me, — for I am your King,
And I have proved myself among you all
An architect. Therefore you will not say,
"This is the voice of failure!" — Yet I know
That you will find some other things to say
Not half so true! For, when a man is old,

> He knows at least how utterly himself
> Has failed! But say what things of me you will
> And be assured I sympathize! Indeed,
> A voice like mine is no-wise terrible,
> As might be the tremendous voice of truth
> Should it find speech that you could understand.
> Yet it may vex and dreadfully distress
> Reflective men, — if such indeed there be
> Among you all, — and therefore be assured,
> I sympathize!

With that, Creon names Herakles as his successor, and the crowd departs, leaving the family surrounding Herakles and congratulating him, until Herakles, breaking away, turns fiercely on the king with passionate reproaches for sacrificing him to selfish politics: —

> Is this your wisdom, Sire? and is it wise,
> Lightly, and thus with calm complacency,
> Now to believe that I, that Herakles
> Should hold himself so cheaply as your price?

The unshaped, mystical consciousness of a destiny to become the Savior, not the Servant, — the creator, not the economist, — the source itself, not the conduit for "these safe human mediocrities," — forces Herakles to reject the crown. He will be

fettered by none of these ties to common, casual
supremacies: —

> Sire, I will not serve the Gods or you!
> Sire, I will not rule by grace of God
> Or by your grace! I will be Lord of none,
> And thus unto myself be Lord and Law!

Therewith the inexorable, tragic succession of
sacrifices, insanities, begins. The dramatist follows up each step in the rising intensities of the
theme, with almost as much care as though he were
a professional alienist. He builds his climax from
the ground, — that is to say, from the family,
which is always the first sacrifice in these mystical
ideals of the Savior. The first of the scenes is laid
at night before the house of Herakles, who listens
to Megara within, singing her children to sleep: —

> My children sleep, whose lives fulfil
>   The soul's tranquillity and trust;
>   While clothed in life's immortal dust
> The patient earth lies dark and still.
>
> All night they lie against my breast
>   And sleep, whose dream of life begins;
>   Before the time of strife and sins,
> Of tears and truth, they take their rest.

The next scene is laid before a tavern door, at
dawn, where Herakles, in his sleepless wandering,
stops to listen to the men and women carousing
within. The poet is heard singing: —

> I know not what it is appears
> To us so worth the tragic task: —
> I know beneath his ribald masque
> Man's sightless face is grey with tears! ›

This tavern scene, to readers who know their
drama of sacrifice and redemption, "is grey with
tears"; and the more because, true to tradition, it
is the woman who first recognizes the Savior, and
putting an end to his anguish of doubt and self-
distrust, draws him on to his fated duty of self-
immolation. The messenger from Eurystheus ar-
rives, while Herakles is parting from his wife and
children, bringing the order to submit to the King
of Argos and the gods, to perform the imposed
labors, and to remain a subject man; but the action of the drama is interrupted here by a discussion between Creon and the poet, of the drama
itself, — the dilemma of Herakles, — a discussion
which is, in a way, more dramatic than the drama

because it broadens the interest to embrace humanity altogether. Like the chorus of Okeanids in Æschylus, Creon sees the hero, and admires him, but doubts what good will come of him to man. He lays down the law, as a King and a Judge must: —

> Crowds are but numbers; and at last I see
> There are not merely players of the game;
> There is not, high or low, only the one
> Sensible and substantial prize, to which
> The fiat of the world gives currency,
> And which, in various ways, is always won!
> There is, besides, the one, estranged, rare man,
> Whose light of life is splendid in the soul,
> Burns with a kind of glory in his strength,
> And gives such special grandeur to ambition
> That he will make no terms with fortune. . . .

Creon's reply to this "estranged, rare man," is that "all men living are not ever free," and that, if not pliant, they are broken. In a dozen lines, as terse as those of Æschylus, he sums up the law of life: —

> Life, like a candle in a starless night,
> Brightens and burns, or flutters and is spent,
> As man's wise weakness spares the guarded flame,

Or man's rash strength resolves in all despite
To lift his torch into the spacious winds,
To blaze his path across the darknesses,
And force the elements to his own undoing . . .
Only the strong go forward — and are slain!
Only the strong, defenceless, dare — and die!
Only the strong, free, fain and fearless — fail!
Remember this! lest a worse thing than mere
Passion and ecstasy of poems befall you!

"Listen to me," says Mercury to Prometheus, at the close of the same dispute in Æschylus; "When misfortune overwhelms you, do not accuse fate; do not upbraid Zeus for striking you an unfair blow! Accuse no one but yourself! You know what threatens you! No surprise! No artifice! Your own folly alone entangles you in these meshes of misery which never release their prey." Creon, as a wise judge, was bound to repeat this warning, and the Poet — in the poem — makes but an unconvincing answer to it, — in fact, loses his temper altogether, until both parties end, as usual, by becoming abusive, in spite of Creon's self-control.

The action of the play repeats the motive of the dialogue. Herakles is exasperated by the insolence of the messenger, to the point of striking him, and threatening to destroy his master. Then, over-whelmed by the mortification of having yielded to a degraded human passion, and of having sunk to the level of the servitude against which he had rebelled, he sets out, in fury and despair, to challenge the oracle of the God at Delphi.

The scene in the temple of Apollo at Delphi follows, where Herakles drags the Pythia from her shrine, and finds himself suddenly saluted as the God.

THE PYTHIA

Yours is the resurrection and the life!

HERAKLES

I am the God!

THE PYTHIA

There is no God but I!
I am whatever is!
I am despair and hope and love and hate,
Freedom and fate,
Life's plangent cry, Death's stagnant silences!
I am the earth and sea and sky,
The race, the runner and the goal; —
There is no thought nor thing but I!

To the ecstasy of the Pythia, the chorus responds in the deepest tones of despair: —

> Have we not learned in bitterness to know
> It matters nothing what we deem or do,
> Whether we find the false or seek the true,
> The profit of our lives is vain and small ?
> Have we not found, whatever price is paid,
> Man is forever cheated and betrayed ?
> So shall the soul at last be cheated after all!

"Coward and weak and abject," is the rejoinder of Herakles, who rises at last to the full consciousness of his divine mission and of the price he must pay for it: —

> I am resolved! And I will stand apart,
> Naked and perfect in my solitude
> Aloft in the clear light perpetually,
> Having afforded to the uttermost
> The blood-stained, tear-drenched ransom of the soul!
> Having by sacrifice, by sacrifice
> Severed his bondage and redeemed the God!
> The God I am indeed! For man is slain,
> And in his death is God illustrious
> And lives!

Then follows the Tenth Scene, the killing of the children. On this, the poet has naturally thrown his

greatest effort, and his rank and standing as a
dramatist must finally rest on it. The reader had
best read it for himself; it is hardly suited to ex-
tracts or criticism; but perhaps, for his own con-
venience, he had better read first the same scene
as Euripides rendered it. This is one of the rare
moments of the dramatic art where more depends
on the audience than on the poet, for the violence
of the dramatic motive — the Sacrifice — carries
the action to a climax beyond expression in words.
The ordinary reader shrinks from it; the tension of
the Greek drama overstrains him; he is shocked at
the sight of an insane man killing his children with
arrows, and refuses to forgive the dramatist for
putting such a sight before him. Insanity has always been the most violent of tragic motives, and
the insanity of Herakles surpassed all other insanities, as the Crucifixion of Christ surpassed all other
crucifixions. Naturally, the person who objects to
the Crucifixion as a *donnée* of the drama, is quite
right in staying away from Ober-Ammergau; but
if he goes to Ober-Ammergau, he must at least
try to understand what the drama means to the

audience, which feels — or should feel — itself en-
globed and incarnated in it. The better-informed
and the more accomplished the critic may be,
who reads the "Herakles" for the first time,
knowing nothing of the author, the more disconcerted he is likely to be in reading it a second
time. His first doubts of the poet's knowledge or
merits will be followed by doubts of his own.

In one respect at least, as a question of dramatic
construction, the doubt is well founded. Critics
object to the "Herakles" of Euripides that it consists of two separate dramas. The same objection
applies to the myth itself. The Savior — whether
Greek, or Christian, or Buddhist — always represents two distinct motives — the dramatic and
the philosophic. The dramatic climax in the
Christian version is reached in the Crucifixion; the
philosophic climax, in the Resurrection and Ascension; but the same personal ties connect the whole
action, and give it unity. This is not the case either
with Herakles or Buddha. The climax of the Greek
version is reached in the killing of the children, so
far as the climax is dramatic; while the philoso-

phic climax — the attainment — is proved by the freeing of Prometheus; and these two *données* are dramatically wide apart, — in fact, totally unconnected. Critics are Creons, and object to being tossed from one motive to another, with an impatient sense of wrong. As drama, one idea was capable of treatment; the other was not.

Probably, the ordinary reader might find an advantage in reading the Twelfth Scene of "Herakles," — the Prometheus, — as a separate poem. After the violent action of killing the children, the freeing of Prometheus seems cold and unconvincing; much less dramatic than the raising of Lazarus or even the Ascension. The Greek solution of this difficulty seems to be known only through fragments of the lost "Prometheus Unbound" of Æschylus, which are attached to most good editions of the poet. Lodge's solution is the necessary outcome of his philosophy, and is worth noting, if for no other reason, because it is personal to him, — or, more exactly, to his Oriental and Schopenhauer idealism. Possibly — perhaps one might almost say probably — it is — both as logic and as history — the more correct solution; but on that point, historians and metaphysicians are the proper sources of authority. Literature has no right to interfere, least of all to decide a question disputed since the origin of thought.

The "Prometheus Unbound" — the Twelfth Scene of " Herakles" — opens, then, upon the Attainment. Herakles has, by self-sacrifice, made himself — and the whole of humanity within him — one with the infinite Will which causes and maintains the universe. He has submitted to God by merging himself in God; he has, by his so-called labors, or miracles, raised humanity to the divine level. Æschylus puts in the mouth of Prometheus the claim to have freed man from the terrors of death and inspired him with blind hopes: "And a precious gift it is that you have given them," responds the chorus! Lodge puts the claim into the mouth of Herakles, and with it his own deification: —

> Not in vain, out of the night of Hell,
> I drew the Hound of Hell, the ravening Death,
> Into the light of life, and held him forth

Where the soul's Sun shed lightnings in his eyes,
And he was like a thing of little meaning,
Powerless and vain and nowise terrible. —
While with my inmost heart I laughed aloud
Into the blind and vacant face of Death,
And cast him from me, so he fled away
Screaming into the darkness whence he came!
Nothing is vain of all that I have done!
I have prevailed by labors, and subdued
All that man is below his utmost truth,
His inmost virtue, his essential strength,
His soul's transcendent, one pre-eminence!
Yea, I have brought into the soul's dominion
All that I am! — and in the Master's House
There is no strength of all my mortal being
That does not serve him now; there is no aim,
There is no secret which He does not know;
There is no will save one, which is the Lord's!

The Church had said the same thing from the beginning; and the Greek, or Oriental, or German philosophy changed the idea only in order to merge the universe in man instead of merging man in the universe. The Man attained, not by absorption of himself in the infinite, but by absorbing the infinite and finite together, in himself, as his own Thought, — his Will, —

> Giving to phases of the senseless flux,
> One after one, the soul's identity;

so that the philosophic climax of the "Prometheus Unbound" suddenly developed itself as a Prometheus bound in fetters only forged by himself; fetters of his own creation which never existed outside his own thought; and which fell from his limbs at once when he attained the force to will it. Prometheus is as much astonished at his own energy as though he were Creon, and, in a dazed and helpless way, asks what he is to do with it: —

> I stand in the beginning, stand and weep.
> Here in the new, bleak light of liberty . . .
> And who am I, and what is liberty?

The answer to this question is that liberty, in itself, is the end, — the sufficient purpose of the will. This simple abstract of the simple thought is the theme of the last speech of Herakles on the last page of the drama: —

> When the long life of all men's endless lives,
> Its gradual pregnancies, its pangs and throes,
> Its countless multitudes of perished Gods
> And outworn forms and spent humanities, —

When all the cosmic process of the past
Stands in the immediate compass of our minds;
When all is present to us, and all is known,
Even to the least, even to the uttermost,
Even to the first and last, — when, over all,
The widening circles of our thought expand
To infinite horizons everywhere, —
Then, tenoned in our foothold on the still,
Supernal, central pinnacle of being,
Shall we not look abroad and look within,
Over the total Universe, the vast,
Complex and vital sum of force and form
And say in one, sufficient utterance,
The single, whole, transcendent Truth, — "I am!"

Not only philosophers, but also, and particularly, society itself, for many thousands of years, have waged bloody wars over these two solutions of the problem, as Prometheus and Herakles, Buddha and Christ, struggled with them in turn: but while neither solution has ever been universally accepted as convincing, that of Herakles has at least the advantage of being as old as the oldest, and as new as the newest philosophy, — as familiar as the drama of the Savior in all his innumerable forms, — as dramatic as it is familiar, —

as poetic as it is dramatic, — and as simple as sacrifice. Paradox for paradox, the only alternative
— Creon's human solution — is on the whole
rather more paradoxical, and certainly less logical,
than the superhuman solution of Herakles.

CHAPTER IX

THE END

This is the whole story! What other efforts Lodge might have made, if he had lived into another phase of life, the effort he had made in this first phase was fatal and final. He rebelled against admitting it, — refused to see it, — yet was conscious that something hung over him which would have some tragic end. Possibly the encouragement of great literary success might have helped and stimulated the action of the heart, but he steeled himself against the illusion of success, and bore with apparent and outward indifference the total indifference of the public. As early as September 30, 1907, he wrote to Marjorie Nott: "I am, for one thing, — and to open a subject too vast to be even properly hinted at here, — drawing to the close of the immense piece of work which has held and compelled me for a year past. The end looms large in my prospect and I am doing my

best, — as you shall one day see. You, in fact, will
be one of only a half-dozen, at best, who will see it.
Which is, I imagine, all to my credit; and certainly
as much as I reasonably want. What I have
learned in the last year, through the work and the
days, I shall never live to express; which is, I take
it, illustrative — as so much else is — of the radi-
cal inferiority of writing your truth instead of
being and living it, — namely that by writing you
can never, at all, keep abreast of it, but inevitably
fall more and more behind as your pace betters.
So I shall eventually perish having consciously
failed, with (like Esmé) 'all my epigrams in me.'
I wonder if Jesus consciously failed; I don't mean,
of course, his total, obvious, practical failure,
which the world for so long has so loudly recorded
in blood and misery and ruin; I mean, did he have
that consciousness of personal, solitary failure,
which one can hardly, with one's utmost imagination, dissociate from the religious being of the soul
of man? I believe he did, — though perhaps his
mind was too simple and single, — as, to some
extent, apparently, was the mind of Socrates. I

sometimes think that the peasant of genius is, perhaps, more outside our comprehension than any other type of man. I perceive that I moon, vaguely moon, — and I shall soon be boring you."

In June, 1908, he went abroad with his mother and father, for change and rest, but his letters show a growing sense of fatigue and effort. To his wife he wrote from the steamer, before landing in England: —

"Our own voyage has come so warmly, so beautifully, back to me in these tranquil sea-days, our own so clear and fine and high adventure into strange new ways, our great adventure which is still in the making. It seems to me, that gay glad beginning, so alone and so one as we were, as something, now, inexpressibly candid and lovely, and humanly brave. And since then, how much, how really much of our young, our confident and defiant boast, — flung, at that time, so happily, and so, after all, grandly, at large, — has been proved and greatened and amplified!"

From London, in July: "London has given

me a new sense of itself, a flavor of romance and
adventure, and the pervading sense of a great,
dingy charm. Yes! it's all been quite new to me,
and wonderfully pleasant; which just satisfac-
torily means, I surmise, that I come all new to it,
— unimpeded by unimportant prejudices, and
prepared vastly more than I was, for life in all its
varieties and interests."

Later, from Paris: "I've lunched and dined
everywhere; I've been to what theatre there is, and
chiefly I've drifted about the streets. And I find
essentially that I seem to demand much more of
life than I ever did, and in consequence take it all
here with a less perfect gayety and a more intense
reflection. I feel matured to an incredible degree,
— as if I did now quite know the whole of life; and
when one's matured, really matured, there is, I
imagine, not much ahead except work. So, back to
you and to work I'm coming soon."

In August, again from Paris: "This whole
Paris experience has been queer and wonderful.
Joe and you have been with me in all the familiar
streets and places, and my youth has appeared to

me in colors richer and more comprehensible than ever before. . . . "

He came home, and brought out "Herakles" in November. In reply to a letter of congratulation from Marjorie Nott, he wrote to her, on December 17: "Thank you! You know that I write for myself, of course, and then, as things are in fact, just for you and so few others. Which is enough! and sees me, so to speak, admirably through. Well! I'm glad you like it, and if you ever have anything more to say of it, you know, my dear, that I want to hear it. You'll find it, of course, long; and you'll strike, I guess, sandy places. Perhaps, though, there are some secrets in it, and some liberties. . . ."

Six months afterwards he took up the theme again, in the last few days of his life, making Marjorie Nott his confidant, as he had done since childhood.

He wrote from Nahant July 31, 1909: —

"Before all else I must thank you, my dear, for the grave and deep emotions roused within me by your letter with its fine, clear note of serious trust and loving favor towards me. Than just that, there

is n't for me anything better to be had. I derive
from it precisely the intimate encouragement
which one so perpetually wants and so exception-
ally gets. Moreover, in all your letter I don't find
a word with which I can possibly disagree. It oc-
curs to me that there may have been, in my pages
to you, some note of complaint, which, in sober
truth, I did n't intend and don't feel. Every man
of us has the Gods to complain of; every man of us,
sooner or later, in some shape, experiences the
tragedy of life. But that, too obviously, is nothing
to cry about, for the tragedy of life is one thing, and
my tragedy or yours, his or hers, is another. All of
us must suffer in the general human fate, and some
must suffer of private wrongs. I've none such to
complain of. At all events, I don't, as I said before, disagree with a word of your letter, but I do,
my dear, find it dreadfully vague. You surely
can't doubt that I deeply realize the value of
human communion of any sort; but that does n't
take me far toward getting it. As I understand
your letter it says to me: 'Well! you might get
more and better if you tried more and better!'

Perhaps! at any rate, goodness knows I do try —
and more and more — as best I can. And surely I
don't complain of the solitude, which has, of course,
its high value; but I do, inevitably, well know it's
there. I 'll spare you more."

His letters to Langdon Mitchell expressed the
same ideas, with such slight difference of form as
one naturally uses in writing to a man rather than
to a woman: —

TO LANGDON MITCHELL

WASHINGTON (*Spring*, 1906).

Thank you, my dear Langdon, for your kind and
so welcome letters. I want to thank you for your
generous offer of help should I try my hand at a
play. . . .

I should have but one personal advantage in
writing a play, namely a genuine indifference as to
its being played or being successful if played. I call
this an advantage because it eliminates the possibility of my mind being disturbed and my powers
consequently impaired by any influences external
to myself. I become so increasingly convinced that
precisely as perfection of being consists in a per-

fectly transparent reality, so artistic perfection
depends upon the degree to which the artist speaks
his own words in his own voice and is unhampered
by the vocabulary of convention and the mega-
phone of oratory — which exists and could exist
only on the theory of an omnipresent multitude.
Let any man speak his own word and he is as
original as Shakespeare and as permanently interesting as Plato. The whole core of the struggle,
for ourselves and for art, is to emerge from the
envelope of thoughts and words and deeds which
are not our own, but the laws and conventions
and traditions formed of a kind of composite of
other men's ideas and emotions and prejudices.
Excuse this dissertation! . . .

Your first letter interested me profoundly, for
my winter has been curiously similar to yours as
you describe it. I have had very poignantly the
same sense of growth, of a revelation and of a con-
sequent observable process of maturity. When
shall we meet and make some exchange of
thoughts? It seems absurd that so great a ma-
jority of my life should be spent without you.

I've been asked (peals of Homeric and scornful laughter from Mitchell) to deliver the poem at the Phi Beta Kappa in Cambridge this spring — June. (Mitchell chokes with mirth and shows symptoms of strangulation. Is patted on the back and recovers. Lodge then good-naturedly continues:) You observe how low I've sunk and for a punishment for your superior sneers I'm going to send you my poem for the occasion to read and criticise. (Mitchell sourly admits that the joke is not entirely on Lodge.) I shall send it soon, in fact it may arrive any day. So I hope that your condition of health is improved.

WASHINGTON, 2346 MASSACHUSETTS AVE.
(*Winter*, 1908).

MY DEAR, DEAR LANGDON, — I shall never have words and ways enough to thank you for your letter. What it meant, what it means to me — the encouragement, the life, the hope — and above all the high felicities of friendship — all these things and other and more things, which you, my dear friend, of your abundance so liberally afford, have enriched and fortified me beyond expression. . . .

My Herakles is done to the last three scenes and hastens somewhat to its end. I won't write you about it, for there is too much to say and finally you'll have to read it — however much it's long and dull.

It's too, too bad you should have been having such a devil's time with this world. But, good heavens, I know what it is to wait; how intolerable it may become sometimes just holding on. But the muscles of patience and that true daily courage which patience implies are fine muscles to have well developed even at some cost — is n't this so, dear man? The living bread and the consecrated wine must be earned and eaten day by day and day by day; we are not made free of perfection by any sudden moment's violence of virtue; the key of the gate of Paradise is not purchased in any single payment however heavy; the travail of God's nativity within us is gradual and slow and laborious. It is the sustained courage, the long stern patience, the intensest daily labor, the clear, per-

petual vigilance of thought, the great resolve,
tranquil and faithful in its strength, — it is these
things, it is the work in short, the wonderful slow
work of man about the soul's business, which ac-
complishes constantly — as we both know so well
— some real thing which makes us, however gradually, other and nobler and greater than we are,
because precisely it makes us more than we are.
All of which you know better than I, for better
than I you do the work and reap the result. But
it's a truth none the less which takes time to learn
— if it is ever learned at all — for the temptation
to think that the reward, the advance is to-morrow,
and that Paradise is in the next county, and that
both can be got by some adventurous extravagance, some single, tense deed of excellence, is very
great, I imagine, to us all. We never realize quite
at once that only patience can see us through, and
that if the moment is not eternity and the place
not Paradise it must be just because we are busy
about what is not, in the true strict test, our real
concern.

WASHINGTON, 2346 MASSACHUSETTS AVE.
(*Spring*, 1908).

O! MY DEAR LANGDON, — Your letter thrilled
and moved me beyond expression. If I do not
thank you for it it is because it has roused within
me emotions nobler and more profound than grati-
tude; and it is in the glamour and power of these
emotions — which will remain permanently inter-
fused with all that I am — that I now write to you.
I tried to read your letter aloud to B. but it moved
me so much and to such depths that I was unable
to continue. This may seem strange to you, for you
will not have thought of all that it means to me;
you will not have been aware of the bare fact that,
apart from the immense inward satisfaction which
the effort of expression must always bring, your
letter is just all of real value I shall get for "Herakles." And it is more, my dear friend, far more
than enough! That is certain. I speak to you with
an open heart and mind, which your letter has liberated, restored, revived, nourished and sustained.
You know as well as I how passionately we have
understanding and sympathy for what is best and

noblest within us. The conception of God the
Father, I believe, came from this longing in the
human heart. But the habit of solitude and silence,
which in this queer country, we perforce assume,
ends by making us less attentive to the heart's
need, and it is only when we are fed that we realize
how consuming was our hunger. For all that is
not what we at best and most truly are, we find
recognition enough, but the very soul within us is
like a solitary stranger in a strange land — and
your letter was to me like a friendly voice speaking
the words of my own tongue and like the lights of
welcome. It is perhaps your criticisms that I re-
joice in most, for I know them to be valid and just.
I feel the faults you find as you feel them, I believe;
and I keep alive the hope that I may learn to feel
them with sufficient force and clearness to correct
them. It would be of infinite advantage to me if
you would, some day, go over the whole thing
with me in detail. Nothing could so much improve my chances of better work in the future.
In fact it would be to me the most essential assistance that I could possibly receive; for if I had you

there to put your finger on the dreadful Saharas
and other undeniable shortcomings, it would illuminate my understanding as nothing else could
do. . . .

Just one thing more. It was a noble act of friendship for you to write me that letter amid all the
labors of your present days. Thanks for that with
all my heart.

With this single condition, the happy life went
on, filled with affection and humor to the end, as
his last letters tell: —

TO HIS MOTHER

NAHANT, *June* 13, 1909.

Our train was seven hours late to Boston, which
fact, when in the East River, after four hours of
open sea, at 6:30 A. M., and by the dull glare of the
hot sun through a white fog, it first gradually and
at last with agonizing completeness possessed my
mind, produced in that sensitive organ emotions
too vivid to be here described.

I had retired to rest reconciled, or at least
steeled, to the thought of a two hours' delay in our

journey; and when, on waking (abysmal moment!) in the squalor of my berth I found that the fog had changed the two hours' delay to seven, I felt in the first shock, other emotions besides surprise. . . . Before emerging in unwashed squalor from my section, I had determined, however, in view of everything, to suppress my feelings and to be, for my poor good children and their nurses, just the requisite hope, cheer and comfort — and this determination (it was the one consoling event of the dreadful day) I did, to the end, successfully carry out. Well, when at last from that dreadful boat we were jerkily drawn once more onto firm land, we fell of course inevitably into the mean hands of the N. Y., N. H. and H. R. R., which characteristically decided that it would, of course, be both cheaper and easier, to give us, instead of the dining car to which — Heaven knows — we seemed entitled, a "fifteen minutes for refreshments" at New Haven; and there, at ten o'clock, in the heartbreaking, dingy dreadfulness of the waiting-room, we — that is the passengers of that luckless train — thronged four deep round a vastly rectangular barrier like a shop-counter, girdled, for the public, by high, greasy, "fixed" stools, covered with inedible pseudo-foods under fly-blown glass bells, and defended, so to speak, by an insufficient and driven horde of waiters and waitresses. You can imagine what chance there was *dans cette galère* for the babes! Fraülein and the nurse secured, by prodigious exertions, and wonderfully drank, cups of a dim grey fluid which they believed to be coffee, while I and the children got back to the train with some apples, oranges, and sinister sandwiches, which all, later, and with every accompanying degradation of drip and slop and grease, all mixed with car dirt, we did devour, — to avoid starvation. I was still further, however, to be in a position to appreciate the exquisite benefits of a railroad monopoly, for when at last our interminable journey did end at Boston, we found, of course, no porters! And with a heavy microscope, book, coat and cane, my three poor unceasingly good, weary and toy-laden children, and my two weary and child-laden nurses, were, perforce, obliged to leave our four bags on the platform, in charge of the

well-feed train porter, to be immediately "called
for" by Moore's man. Which man, young Moore
himself, I duly found and straitly charged about
the four bags, as well as about my seven pieces
in the "van." Then, somewhat cheered, and having renewed to Moore (who, as you will presently
perceive, I have come to regard as an abysmal
though quite well-intentioned young ass) my
charge as to the four bags, I drove off to the
North Station, stopping en route merely to reward
my lambs for their exemplary conduct by a rubber
toy apiece. Well! at that point, I think you will
agree with me that the wariest might have been
lulled into a sense that the worst was over and
plain sailing ahead. Such at least was my condition of confidence, and though in the North Station waiting-room, our bedraggled, dirty, worn-
out company waited a full hour for Moore and
the trunks, I just put it down as evidence that
the benefits of the railroad we had just left were
still accumulating, and hoped on. And then Moore
arrived — arrived, having just merely forgotten
the four bags — having in short left them — one

of them containing Uncle Henry's manuscript and
all of mine, both irreplaceable — just there on the
platform where I could n't have not left them.
Well! for a moment I did n't "keep up" a bit
and addressed to Moore a few — how inadequate!
— "feeling words."   I then dispatched him back
to recover the bags, packed my poor babes into
the 3:20 for Lynn, — trusting, as I had to, to
Fraülein's ability to get them out at Lynn, — and
remained myself at the North Station, where I
waited for Moore for exactly one hour and fifteen
minutes. My state of mind I won't describe. At
the end of that vigil, however, I mounted — always with microscope, book, coat and cane — in a
taxicab, went to the South Station, found Moore,
and after an interval of almost panic, when I
thought all the manuscripts were lost for good,
did, by dint of energy at last — thank Heaven —
find the bags. . . . Well! I felt then a little "gone"
and went therefore to the Club, had a drink and a
sandwich, just in time, and got, at last, to Nahant,
at about seven o'clock, to find that, by some mistake, they had given me, for the nurse's bag, the

bag of a total stranger. In the nurse's bag was, beside her own effects, some of Helena's, including a silver mug; and so as I lay, at last, in my bath I heard, strangely concordant with my whole horrible day's experience, Fraülein and Hedwig mourning, in shrill German, the loss. So Monday, I go to town to do some errands and to find if possible the damned bag. The children are none the worse for the journey and are already benefited by the good air. The house is incredibly clean and charming and we are delighted with it.

TUCKANUCK, *July*, 1909.

I am having the most beautiful days — endless air and sea and sun and beauty, and best of all with Langdon's splendid companionship. It's all just what I've wanted and needed for so long. I have shown Langdon my latest work, — "The Noctambulist," etc., — what I read to you in Washington, — and he is most splendidly encouraging. He feels as strongly as I could wish that I have made, both in thought and form, a really new and large and valid departure. Which endlessly cheers me, as you will believe. We talk together of everything first and last, off and on, but chiefly on, all day and night with the exception of many hours of sleep. I do no work and just take easily all my present blessings as greedily as I can.

Langdon Mitchell was one of the half-dozen readers, as he said, for whose approbation he wrote, and this last companionship with him at Tuckanuck in July, gave Lodge keen pleasure. On returning to Nahant he wrote to Sturgis Bigelow, who was then ill in Paris: —

"I've just returned home from Tuckanuck, browned to the most beautiful color by ten glorious days of sun. Langdon and I went together, and except for one day of warm, sweet rain, and one morning of fog, — which cleared splendidly in time for the bath, — we had weather of uninterrupted magnificence. Immeasurable sky and sea and sun, warm water, hot clean sand, clear light, transparent air, — Tuckanuck at its perfect best. I've returned made over in mind and body, feeling better in every way than I've felt since I can remember. For this I have to thank you, for Tuckanuck, — and Langdon for his wonderful, interesting, vital companionship. Together — with every variety of the best talk, the finest communion — we lived all day and night long immersed in the beneficent elements, the prodigious light and air, the sounding, sparkling, flowing sea; and the bathing was different and better every day. The sea showed us all its loveliest moods. On one day it was stretched and smooth to the horizon, drawn away from the shore, on a light north wind, in endless fine blue wrinkles, with just the merest crisp, small ripple on the beach. Another day, fresh southwest wind, with a fine, high, lively, light surf. And even on one day the biggest waves of the season — too big for comfort. Well! it was all glorious; — you will understand; we have had it just like that so often together. Indeed your presence was the one thing we longed for, and did n't have, throughout our whole visit. There was hardly an hour down there when I did n't think of you and long for you. . . . Never had I more needed the restorative

magic of nature and companionship than when
I set forth for that blessed island, and never did it
more wonderfully work upon me its beneficent
spell. To judge by the way I feel now, I have n't
known what it was to be really rested and well
since I finished 'Herakles.' I feel pages more of
enthusiasm at the end of my pen, but I will spare
you. I took down to the island with me my winter's work, which has taken the shape of a volume
of poems ready for publication, and read it to
Langdon, who, thank goodness, felt high praise
for them — more enthusiastic approval, indeed,
than I had dared to hope for."

Langdon Mitchell's encouragement and sympathy were pathetically grateful to him, so rare
was the voice of an impartial and competent judge.
He wrote to his wife in the warmest appreciation
of it.

|"I have been having such good days! Langdon
is of course the utmost delight to me, and the
presence of companionship day by day is fresh
and wonderful to me beyond measure. Also the
weather in general has been glorious, and the whole

spectacle of the world clothed in light and beauty.
I lead a sane and hygienic life. We go to bed before
twelve, and sleep all we can. We breakfast, read,
write perhaps an occasional letter, talk for long,
fine, clear stretches of thought, and regardless of
time, play silly but active games on the grass,
swim, bask in the sun, sail, and talk, and read
aloud, and read to ourselves, and talk, and talk.
. . . I'm getting into splendid condition."

When his father, fagged by the long fatigues of
the tariff session, returned north, they went back
to Tuckanuck together in August, and there he
had the pleasure of a visit from a new and enthusiastic admirer, Mr. Alfred Brown, lecturer and
critic, who brought him for the first time a sense
of possible appreciation beyond his personal
friends.

He never alluded to his own symptoms. Even
his father, though on the watch, noticed only that
he spared himself, and took more frequent rests.
To Sturgis Bigelow he wrote of his anxiety about
both Bigelow and his father, whom, he said, he
was helping to "get his much-needed rest and re-

cuperation, and I think he is getting them, both, good and plenty, but the knowledge that you will probably not get here this season makes the dear island seem singularly deserted. . . . It's all doing him good, and what is more, he thinks it is. . . . I read a good deal, and take my swim, and an occasional sail. Also, after a month's vacation during which I haven't written a line, I've now begun again, and write and meditate for four or five hours every day . . . so that life flows evenly and quietly and cheerfully. Still, lacking the stimulus of your prospective arrival, I shan't be sorry to get back to my Pussy and my babes."

This seems to have been one of the last letters he wrote. It was mailed at Nantucket, August 18, and on the 19th he was seized at night by violent indigestion, probably due to some ptomaine poison. The next day he was better. The distress returned on the night of the twentieth. Twenty-four hours of suffering ensued ; then the heart suddenly failed and the end came.

𝕬𝕳𝖊 𝕽𝖎𝖛𝖊𝖗𝖘𝖎𝖉𝖊 𝕻𝖗𝖊𝖘𝖘
CAMBRIDGE . MASSACHUSETTS
U . S . A